# Film Noir

D0995130

Stanley Kubrick
Martin Scorsese
Noir Fiction
Alfred Hitchcock

As Martin Fitzgerald
Orson Welles
Hong Kong's Heroic Bloodshed
Woody Allen

www.pocketessentials.com

# Film Noir

## Paul Duncan

www.pocketessentials.com

This edition published in 2006 by Pocket Essentials
P.O.Box 394, Harpenden, Herts, AL5 1XJ
www.pocketessentials.com

© Paul Duncan 2000, 2003, 2006

The right of Paul Duncan to be identified as the author of this work has been
asserted in accordance with the Copyright, Designs and Patents Act 1988.

All rights reserved. No part of this book may be reproduced, stored
in or introduced into a retrieval system, or transmitted, in any form
or by any means (electronic, mechanical, photocopying, recording or
otherwise) without the written permission of the publishers.

Any person who does any unauthorised act in relation to this publication
may be liable to criminal prosecution and civil claims for damages.

A CIP catalogue record for this book is available from the British Library.

ISBN  1 904048 67 6
EAN 978 1 904048 67 1

2  4  6  8  10  9  7  5  3  1

Typeset by Avocet Typeset, Chilton, Aylesbury, Bucks
Printed and bound in Great Britain by Cox & Wyman, Reading

For Claude and Josef

# Acknowledgements

Thanks are due to the ever-resourceful Ellen Cheshire for lending me various books and videos from her collection. For the first edition I relied heavily on the third edition of *Film Noir: An Encyclopaedic Reference to the American Style* by Alain Silver and Elizabeth Ward, and *Dark City: The Film Noir* by Spencer Selby. For the second edition, I had the pleasure of finding www.noirfilms.com, which I urge you to visit.

As always, merci beaucoup to Claude and Josef, who are the lights that guide me out of the darkness.

# Contents

# Contents

# Film Noir: Films of Trust and Betrayal

'An extraordinary, horrible war. Concentration camps, slaughter, atomic bombs, people killed for nothing. That can make anybody a little pessimistic.'

– Abraham Polonsky

When I think of Film Noir, I think of stillness and silence. I think of a pure black screen with tiny pinpricks of white trying to break through. The image is of the central character thinking. He is thinking about all the bad things that are about to happen to him. He is not happy. He knows that shit happens, but why does it have to happen to him? Film Noir gives him the answer: Why not?

*

This Pocket Essential is designed to be an overview of Film Noir. After defining the different types of Film Noir, there is a short history of its antecedents and development over the years. A few films are examined in depth and then a filmography lists over 1000 Films Noirs, 647 of which are from the Classic Noir Period (1940–1960). Finally, there is a reference section which lists books, articles and websites about Film Noir.

## Definition

The usual relationship in a Film Noir is that the male character (private eye, cop, journalist, government agent, war veteran, criminal, lowlife) has a choice between two women: the beautiful and the dutiful. The dutiful woman is pretty, reliable, always there for him, in love with him, responsible – all the things any real man would dream about. The beautiful woman is the femme fatale, who is gorgeous, unreliable, never there for him, not in love with him, irresponsible – all the things a man needs to get him excited about a woman. The Film Noir follows our hero as he makes his choice, or his choice is made for him.

The reason the femme fatale meets the male character is because she has already made her choice. She is usually involved with an older, very powerful man (gangster, politician, millionaire), and she is looking to make some money from the relationship. She needs a smart man (who is also dumber than her) to go get that money, and take the fall if things go wrong. Enter the male character.

The story follows the romantic/erotic foreplay of their relationship. The male character is often physically and mentally abused in this meeting and separating of bodies. Sometimes, he ends up doing very bad things.

What is most surprising about Film Noir, and the reason I suspect it has become so difficult to categorise and pigeonhole, is that the focus of the films can be from the point of view of any of the characters caught in this relationship. For example, we can follow the femme fatale's story or, as is more often the case, the dutiful woman's. (The timid, unknowing woman who learns about the dark side of life harks back to the Gothic novel of the nineteenth century, which is where Noir Fiction came from.) This is because all the characters are equally interesting – they are all either obsessed with something they desire (money, power, sex), or compelled to do what they do because of their nature, or the physical or social environment they live in.

The Film Noir follows a number of discernible frameworks

within which the characters clash and collide. To show the workings of the police and government agencies, we had the Documentary Noir. Many filmmakers worked with army documentary units during World War Two, and discovered the freedom of movement the new, lightweight cameras afforded them. Audiences back home also got used to seeing them, so they found it easier to accept the rough style when it was presented to them as a feature film. The Docu Noir invariably had an authoritative voice telling us the facts (time, place, purpose) of the case, and we followed the investigation through to the end. The first one was *The House on 92nd Street* (1945) directed by Henry Hathaway, who did several in this style. Others of note include *Call Northside 777* (1948), *The Naked City* (1948) (which spawned a TV series), Joseph H Lewis' *The Undercover Man* (1949) and *The Enforcer* (1951). In the 50s, this style was subverted and reinvented by Alfred Hitchcock in his magnificent *The Wrong Man* (1956). In this film, instead of glorifying the law, we see a man and his family becoming victims of the police procedure – in the end his wife has a mental breakdown.

The Docu Noir ran for about 5 years, and was superseded by the Heist Noir – the meticulously planned robbery that goes horribly wrong. The most well-known of the early ones is probably John Huston's *The Asphalt Jungle* (1950), although *Criss Cross* (1949), directed by Robert Siodmak, preceded it. Others of note include *Armoured Car Robbery* (1950), *The Killing* (1956), *Plunder Road* (1957) and *Odds Against Tomorrow* (1959). In each case, it is a flaw in one of the characters which results in the ultimate come-uppance of the criminals. For example, Johnny Clay in *The Killing* is the professional robber in a gang of novices, yet he loses the money because of his lack of professionalism – he bought a defective case instead of a sturdy one, which leads to the case snapping open on a runway and the money swirling about his getaway plane. (Irony plays a large part in Film Noir.)

The Amnesia Noir, where the central character has no memory of their past, allowed the audience to discover, with the character, what happened in the past. For example, *Street of Chance* (1942), *Crossroads* (1942), *Two o'Clock Courage* (1945), *Somewhere in the Night* (1946), *Fall Guy* (1947), *The Crooked Way* (1949) and *The Long Wait* (1954). Associated with this were the Nightmare Noirs. This is usually the story of a fish out of water, about somebody whose whole life disintegrates in front of their eyes, who watches helplessly as the ground falls away from beneath their feet. Often, the nightmare is combined with a race against time to prove innocence before something really bad happens. Examples include: *The Fallen Sparrow* (1943), *Ministry of Fear* (1944), *My Name is Julia Ross* (1945), *Detour* (1945), *Escape in the Fog* (1945), *Crack-Up* (1946), *The Chase* (1946), *Deadline at Dawn* (1946), *Desperate* (1947), *The Accused* (1949), *DOA* (1950), *Night and the City* (1950), *Side Street* (1950), *Cause for Alarm* (1951), *Nightfall* (1957). Madness can take many forms. Duality is one of the major themes of Film Noir, and it is sometimes explored through the Doppelgänger, or double, in films like *Dark Mirror* (1946), *The Guilty* (1947), *Hollow Triumph* (1948) and *The Man With My Face* (1951).

The 1941 Gangster Noir *High Sierra* (1941) marked a turning point in the representation of the gangster because Roy 'Mad Dog' Earle was seen to be coming to the end of his time. From that moment on, we saw the mental disintegration of the criminal in films like *The Gangster* (1947), *White Heat* (1949) and *Kiss Tomorrow Goodbye* (1950). The emphasis was on the sadism of these powerful men. The Psycho Noir took the idea one step further – the central character is completely bonkers from the start! One of the most well-known is *The Sniper* (1952), but check out *Hangover Square* (1945), *Dial 1119* (1950), *The Hitch-Hiker* (1953) and *The Night Runner* (1957).

When women went psycho, the story was always much more unpredictable, as can be seen in Psychological Noirs like *Dark Waters* (1944), *Guest in the House* (1944), *Possessed* (1947) and *The Red House* (1947). It was rare for a Film Noir to be shown from the point of view of the femme fatale, but Gene Tierney had perhaps her greatest role in *Leave Her to Heaven* (1945), in which she killed her stepson and her unborn child to keep the man she loved.

Love was not always obsessive in Film Noir. Runaway Noir began with Fritz Lang's *You Only Live Once* (1937), when two lovers go on the run because one of them is a criminal. For these youngsters, the purity of their love transcends all the bad things they do. You can follow this thread through to *They Live By Night* (1948), and *Gun Crazy* (1950), and then from *Bonnie and Clyde* (1967) to *Wild at Heart* (1990).

The purity of unconditional love is a theme that also often runs through Gothic and Victorian Noirs like *Rebecca* (1940), where *Jane Eyre*-like, the timid woman blossoms into a confident beauty to win the heart of an initially aggressive master. Or rather, this traditional form is subverted in Film Noir. In *Moss Rose* (1947) a woman blackmails a country gentleman. In *So Evil My Love* (1949) a woman is transformed into a cold-blooded murderess over the course of the story.

But still, in many Films Noirs, the woman remained in danger. *Suspicion* (1941) was one of the first and best of the Woman-in-Distress Noirs, which included *Experiment Perilous* (1944), *Gaslight* (1944, a man tries to drive his wife mad) and the classic *My Name is Julia Ross* (1945). Not content with putting women at risk, Film Noir also enjoyed imperilling children in films like *The Window* (1949), *Talk About a Stranger* (1952), and *The Night of the Hunter* (1955). It is very rare indeed that a child dies – in fact, the only example I can think of is young Stevie being blown up in Alfred Hitchcock's *Sabotage* (1936).

Films Noirs are stories about doomed love set in a criminal or degrading world. From the beginning, we know that things are going to end badly, so the stories take on a tragic dimension. The only question to be asked is how the characters get to that final, horrible moment that we dread.

## History

With the end of World War Two, French publisher Gallimard decided to launch a new imprint to publish the English and American Hard-Boiled novels they could not publish during the war. In August 1945, Série Noire was born. As well as meaning 'The Black Series' the name was also a play on words because 'une série noire' means a succession of bad events. The first 30 titles included works by Raymond Chandler, Horace McCoy, W R Burnett, Dashiell Hammett and others.

Film Noir was discovered by French cinéaste Nino Frank in 1946. It was the name he gave to describe all the American crime and detective films from the early 1940s which had just been released in France. He noticed how dark the films were and Film Noir seemed an appropriate sister term to Série Noire. For many years, Film Noir was a term only used by French film critics, most notably in *Panorama Du Film Noir Américain* (1955) by Raymond Borde & Etienne Chaumeton. The first short survey of these dark films in English was in a chapter of *Hollywood in the Forties* (1968) by Charles Higham & Joel Greenberg. Raymond Durgnat tried to define categories in his article *Paint It Black: The Family Tree of Film Noir* (*Cinema* [UK], August 1970), and then Paul Schrader presented his definitions in the article *Notes of Film Noir* (*Film Comment*, Spring 1972). Since then, many books about Film Noir have been published with lists and definitions for every taste.

The problem, or joy, of Film Noir is that it is not a genre which can be easily defined, but it is a matter of tone and mood, as both Durgnat and Schrader point out. Generally, a Film Noir is pessimistic in tone and reflective in mood, often presented with a voice-over, and a series of flashbacks. The visual image is often made up of layers of black and grey. The characters are obsessed, or are compelled to act in the way they do.

A combination of 1930s influences helped create Film Noir: the German Expressionists; the French Poetic Realists; Hollywood Gangsters; Tough Guy writers.

The look of Film Noir can be traced back to the German Expressionist cinema of the 1920s and 1930s. Although the 'ultimate' example of this cinema is *The Cabinet of Dr Caligari* (1919, d Robert Wiene) with its surreal settings and caricatured people, the emphasis on graphic design, weird angles, montage, forced perspective and other technical innovations was to play a major part in the formation of Film Noir. Also, the Germanic culture paid more attention to the psychology of the characters, and was preoccupied with analysing their actions. They wanted to know what was happening inside people. Fritz Lang's *M* (1931), for example, shows us the points of view of police, criminal underworld and child-killer.

Many film directors and their creative personal escaped Hitler's Germany and hotfooted it to Hollywood. These included Fritz Lang, Billy Wilder, Robert Siodmak, Fred Zinnemann and Edgar G Ulmer. What is not generally acknowledged is that most came via France. Many of the themes and settings of Film Noir can be seen in films of the Poetic Realists of the 1930s.

Poetic realism is a term first applied to the French literature of Emile Zola, Francis Carco and their ilk. It was first applied to films with Pierre Chenal's *La Rue Sans Nom* (1933). These books and films looked at the outside forces affecting people's lives. They used real settings (the city), real people in a social context (the proletariat or lower middle classes) and showed that crime came from physical and mental oppression. The weak-willed protagonist would find himself trapped in a situation created by society, surrounded by a romantic aura of doom and despair.

German filmmakers who visited Paris before heading for Hollywood include Robert Siodmak, Fritz Lang, Billy Wilder, Max Ophüls, Jacques Tourneur and Curtis Bernhardt. Some French directors soon followed (Jean Renoir, Julien Duvivier, Jacques Tourneur). And there is one well-known British director, who served his film apprenticeship in Berlin, who made his way to the City of Angels in 1939: Alfred Hitchcock.

It is not surprising then, that these directors later took the opportunity to remake French, German and British crime films as Films Noirs: *La Chienne* (1931, d Jean Renoir) as *Scarlet Street* (1946, d Fritz Lang); *La Bête Humaine* (1938, d Jean Renoir) as *Human Desire* (1954, d Fritz Lang); *Pépé Le Moko* (1936, d Julien Duvivier) as *Algiers* (1938, d John Cromwell) & *Casbah* (1948, d John Berry); *Le Jour Se Lève* (1939, d Marcel Carné) as *The Long Night* (1947, d Anatole Litvak); *Pièges* (1939, d Robert Siodmak) as *Lured/Personal Column* (1947, d Douglas Sirk); *Le Dernier Tournant* (1939, d Pierre Chenal) as *The Postman Always Rings Twice* (1946, d Tay Garnett); *Le Corbeau* (1943, d Henri-Georges Clouzot) as *The Thirteenth Letter* (1950, d Otto Preminger).

Many of the milieu, characters, icons, actors came from the Hollywood Gangsters. In Depression-era America of the 1930s, the activities of the gangsters were front-page news. They were attractive figures because of their money, power, clothes, status symbols, and women. Hollywood put them on the silver screen in *Little Ceasar* (1930, d Mervyn LeRoy, n W R Burnett, c Edgar G Robinson), *The Public Enemy* (1931, d William A Wellman, c James Cagney) and *Scarface* (1932, d Howard Hawks, sc Ben Hecht, c Paul Muni, George Raft). These were coded warnings. They were often exaggerated rags-to-riches stories about how money and power corrupt people. This was an especially ironic statement because of the lack of money in Depression-era America.

The public outcry from the Legion of Decency and others over the deluge of gangsters portrayed as heroes led to a new twist, the actors playing the gangsters gave the same tough, brutal performances but this time on the side of the law. So audiences hoping that James Cagney was playing a Gangster-Man in *G-Men* (1935, d William Keighley) soon found out he was a Government-Man. Then films like *Dead End* (1937, d William Wyler) and *Angels With Dirty Faces* (1938, d Michael Curtiz) went one step further and showed that crime originated in the slums. The criminal iconography and setting were now firmly imbedded in the minds of the American public.

With the European and American directors in Hollywood, what were they to film? Hollywood primarily films the best-selling books of its time and in the late 1930s and early 1940s these were Hard-Boiled novels by the likes of Dashiell Hammett and Raymond Chandler. This was a macho fiction where tough guys passed moral judgement on an immoral society. As the 1940s progressed, Noir Fiction novels by James M Cain, David Goodis and Cornell Woolrich emerged. These were about the weak-minded, the losers, the bottom-feeders, the obsessives, the compulsives and the psychopaths. Noir shows these people sliding down into the abyss or, if they happen to be in it already, forever writhing, aware of the present pain, aware of the future pain to come.

This was the raw material the directors mined for their work. As luck would have it, many of the Hard-Boiled and Noir Fiction writers lived in Los Angeles and liked making money writing film scripts. The best-known were Daniel Mainwaring (aka Geoffrey Homes, *Build My Gallows High*), Steve Fisher (*I Wake Up Screaming*), Jonathan Latimer (*Solomon's Vineyard*), Horace McCoy (*They Shoot Horses, Don't*

*They?*) and W R Burnett (*Little Caesar, High Sierra, The Asphalt Jungle*).

It should be recognised that the 'gothic' lighting style of Film Noir, and the Expressionist angles, were much in evidence during the silent era. The films of Sergei Eisenstein in Russia, and Tod Browning's horror films in Hollywood, for example. The night-time and location shooting which were common for silent films was impossible with the advent of sound because the equipment was too bulky and noisy. Consequently, the 1930s were a relatively fallow period for dark cinema.

When advances in technology meant that cameras became lighter and more mobile, the cinematographers explored every possibility. Many of the cinematographers (Nicholas Musuraca, George Barnes, Joseph A Valentine, Hal Mohr, John F Seitz, Joseph La Shelle etc) were veterans of the silent era, having began work in the 1910s and 1920s. So they were at the height of their skills when asked to layer light and shadows like they had during the silent days. A quick look at *Rebecca* (1940), for example, shows the camera prowling around Manderley like a wild animal hunting for blood.

In addition, the sparse, single-source lighting style of cinematography which became the norm for Film Noir arose out of necessity. The advent of World War Two meant the sales market for Hollywood movies shrunk enormously. As a result, budgets were reduced, and dark shadows were employed to hide the fact that there was no set. This was certainly the case for B-pictures photographed by John Alton, George E Diskant and others.

Critics argue about which were the first and last Film Noirs of the Classic Period (*Rebecca* [1940] & *Vertigo* [1958], *Stranger on the Third Floor* [1940] & *Odds Against Tomorrow* [1957], *Citizen Kane* [1941] & *Touch of Evil* [1958]), and even argue about the length of the Classic Period (1940–1960,

1945–1955). I let them argue it out and spend the time watching another Film Noir on TV.

During the optimistic 1960s, there was no concerted Film Noir movement to speak of. Hollywood was more interested in worldwide spies and sword & sandal epics. A film like *Point Blank* (1967) came out of nowhere. It wasn't until the early 1970s, when the industry allowed itself to be revitalised by new talent after the success of *Easy Rider*, that we saw *Dirty Harry* (1971), *Klute* (1971), *The Friends of Eddie Coyle* (1973), *Serpico* (1973), *Bring Me the Head of Alfredo Garcia* (1974), *The Parallax View* (1974), *Chinatown* (1974), *The Conversation* (1974), *Death Wish* (1974), *Three Days of the Condor* (1975) and *Night Moves* (1975). These are stories about people who expected more from the world and were disappointed by it. All these films share a certain sense of paranoia, cynicism and pessimism which paved the way for Neo-Noir.

The heavily coded political content of Film Noir arose from both the sensitivity of the German film directors to feelings of oppression, and from the left-wing origins of many of the Hard-Boiled writers. Recent Films Noirs, often called Neo-Noir, have been made by film directors who seem to have no political or sociological standpoint, and seem more interested in style over content. For example, as entertaining as the films of Quentin Tarantino are, they are no more than a collection of references to other films and books. If you look at the work of John Dahl (*Kill Me Again*, *Red Rock West*, *The Last Seduction*) they are reminiscent of *Farewell My Lovely*, *Double Indemnity* and other bygone films. Some films, like *Devil In a Blue Dress* and *LA Confidential* retain the historical setting. *Heat* is Docu Noir. *Face/Off* is Gangster Noir. *The Talented Mr Ripley* is Psychological Noir. *Wild at Heart* is Runaway Noir. *Basic Instinct* is Femme Fatale Noir. *Henry: Portrait of a Serial Killer* is Psycho Noir.

With the republication of Noir Fiction by Jim Thompson,

David Goodis, Cornell Woolrich and others during the mid-1980s, many of these books were snapped up by film producers. As a result, there was an explosion of Neo-Noirs in the early 1990s. Filmmakers have since discovered modern Noir Fiction writers like James Ellroy (*LA Confidential*) and Edward Bunker (*No Beast So Fierce*, *Animal Factory*), and are busy adapting their novels for the big screen. (My companion Pocket Essential volume, *Noir Fiction: Dark Highways*, highlights 19 noir writers.)

★

It is still and silent. The pure black screen has tiny pinpricks of white trying to break through. The central character is thinking. He is thinking about all the bad things that have happened to him. He is not happy. He knows that shit happens, but why did it have to happen to him? He smiles, because he is alive. If he doesn't get killed today, he'll consider it a lucky day.

# In Depth

## Stranger on the Third Floor (1940)

**Cast:** Peter Lorre (The Stranger), John McGuire (Michael 'Mike' Ward), Margaret Tallichet (Jane), Charles Waldron (District Attorney), Elisha Cook Jr (Joe Briggs), Charles Halton (Albert Meng), Ethel Griffies (Mrs. Kane, Michael's Landlady), Cliff Clark (Martin), Oscar O'Shea (The Judge), Alec Craig Briggs (Defense Attorney), Otto Hoffman (Police Surgeon), Bobby Barber (Giuseppe)

**Crew:** Director Boris Ingster, Writers Frank Partos (& Nathanael West), Producer Lee S Marcus, Composer Roy Webb, Cinematographer Nicholas Musuraca, Editor Harry Marker, Art Director Van Nest Polglase, Assistant Director James E Casey, Sound Bailey Fesler, Special Effects Vernon L Walker, 64 mins

**Trustee:** Joe Briggs

**Traitor:** Mike Ward

**Story:** Reporter Mike Ward is happy with his pay rise, because he can now marry Jane and put the down payment on a house for them. At last he can get out of his crummy little third floor apartment. Mike has got the money because he is the star witness in a murder trial – he saw Joe Briggs standing over Giuseppe's body in the coffee shop – which is bringing him money and fame. At the trial, Joe explains that he was returning money he had owed Giuseppe, then panicked and ran when he saw the body. Joe Briggs: 'It wasn't very nice. His throat was cut. Blood was dripping into the open drawer of the cash register.' Listening to the testimony, Mike begins to doubt that Joe is the murderer because all the evidence is circumstantial. Nobody else seems bothered that Joe might get the death penalty – his friend and fellow-reporter Martin tells him, 'There's too many people in the world as it is.'

The jury return their verdict of murder and the judge sentences Joe to death. Jane takes the verdict badly and decides that they should not meet that night. Mike returns to his gloomy apartment and tries to get some sleep. He cannot hear his unpleasant neighbour, Albert Meng, who normally snores. (They met for the first time when Meng complained that Mike's typing was keeping him up at night.) Mike goes out onto the landing to knock on Meng's door. Outside, Mike sees a little man hiding in the shadows, and chases him down the stairs. Returning to his room, Mike thinks that Meng may be dead, but dares not investigate further, because there was one time in Giuseppe's that he complained to Martin about Meng, saying that he could kill the old man. Mike asks, 'Did you ever want to kill a man?' 'My son,' Martin replies, 'There's murder in every intelligent man's heart.' Meng is there, ogling two young women, which prompts Mike to comment, 'He looks as though his mind could stand a little laundering.'

And then there was the other time when Jane came to his room to dry off after a rainstorm. Meng and the landlady burst in and told Jane she had to leave. Mike grabbed hold of Meng and threatened him because he had called the landlady and was taking a long look at Jane's legs. Mike has a nightmare and dreams that with all this circumstantial evidence, a jury would be certain to find him guilty if Meng was dead.

Waking, Mike goes into Meng's room and finds the old man dead. He panics, packs his bag, and then calls Jane to see what money she could give him. Jane persuades Mike to call the police. When they come, the police don't believe Mike saw a man on the stairs. They also find it suspicious that the same man should find two bodies. With Mike arrested on circumstantial evidence, Jane leaves work to search for a small man with protruding eyes, big lips and a white scarf.

After walking the streets all night, and asking everybody with no success, Jane goes into a café to get a coffee. A small man enters and asks, 'I want a couple of hamburgers and I'd like them raw.' Jane follows him and sees him feed the hamburgers to a dog. She begins talking to the man, finds out that he is from an asylum. When she realises she is in danger, she runs away, with the man chasing. He is run over by a truck. The driver pleads with Jane, 'It wasn't my fault. You'll be a witness, won't you?'

With his dying breath, the little man confesses he killed both men. Mike and Jane are free to spend their life together.

**Subtext:** This is a story about Mike assuaging his guilt for the wrong he did Joe Briggs. Mike's newspaper pal Martin represents all those wanting to maintain the status quo by going along with the crowd, whereas Jane is his conscience. It is significant that Jane (a secretary) investigates for Mike instead of his experienced fact-finder friend Martin.

**Dark Visions:** Flashbacks. A shadow outlining a figure. Venetian blinds. Light through staircase spraying shadows over wall.

**White Noise:** Voice-over by Mike for about 20 minutes.

**Dangerous Ideas:** Nightmare Noir. The wrong man being

accused (twice). Dream sequence. Racing against time to save two lives. The sympathetic psychopath (he feeds animals, and is nice to Jane). A woman investigates. The fedora flipped back on the head and the legs up on the table. Plot turned on head (hero goes to jail and girlfriend saves him).

**Background:** Peter Lorre, who made his film debut in Fritz Lang's murder-masterpiece *M* (1931), had only 2 days left on his contract with RKO, so they decided to make the best use of his availability by giving him a few lines in a few scenes. He got top billing!

**The Director:** Boris Ingster (1904–1978) began as a writer in the mid-1930s, graduated to director with *Stranger on the Third Floor*, then returned to writing until he directed two other films, including the Film Noir *Southside 1-1000* (1950). From 1964, he became a producer & writer for *The Man From U.N.C.L.E.* TV series and films.

**The Writers:** Frank Partos also wrote *The House on Telegraph Hill* (1951) and *Night Without Sleep* (1952). Nathanael West wrote the Noir Fiction novels *Miss Lonelyhearts* (1933) and *The Day of the Locust* (1939).

**The Photographer:** Italian Nicholas Musuraca (1892–1975) began his career as a cinematographer with *On the Banks of the Wabash* (1923) and completed 102 films in every genre before working on *Stranger on the Third Floor*. He has densely layered shadows, using venetian blinds and staircase supports to create patterns on the walls. There is also a lot of camera movement. Musuraca went on to photograph many important Films Noirs, working with Lang, Ray, Brahm, Farrow, Tourneur, Siodmak and others.

**The Verdict:** Released the same month as Raoul Walsh's *They Drive By Night*, and four months after Alfred Hitchcock's Gothic Noir *Rebecca*, this is often listed as the first Film Noir because of the German expressionistic photographic style. It also uses three flashbacks, a nightmare dream sequence and turns the story on its head by putting the hero in jail! It is watchable with a few nice sequences and bits of dialogue. 3/5

## *Shadow of a Doubt* (1943)

**Cast:** Teresa Wright (Young Charlie Newton), Joseph Cotten (Charlie Oakley), Macdonald Carey (Jack Graham), Henry Travers (Joseph Newton), Patricia Collinge (Emma Newton), Hume Cronyn (Herbie Hawkins), Wallace Ford (Fred Saunders), Edna Mae Wonacott (Ann Newton), Charles Bates (Roger Newton), Irving Bacon (Station Master), Clarence Muse (Railroad Porter), Janet Shaw (Louise), Estelle Jewell (Girlfriend)

**Crew:** Director Alfred Hitchcock, Screenplay Thornton Wilder, Sally Benson, Alma Reville, Story Gordon McDonell, Producer Jack H Skirball, Original Music Dimitri Tiomkin, Cinematographer Joseph A Valentine, Film Editing Milton Carruth, Art Direction Robert F Boyle, John B Goodman, Assistant Director Ralph Slosser

**Trustee:** Charlie

**Traitor:** Uncle Charlie

**Story:** Charlie is bored with life, complaining that the family is in a rut and that nothing happens in their small town, so she decides to telegraph her Uncle Charlie to come and visit. At the same time, in a decaying city, Uncle Charlie is being pursued by two men, so he decides to visit his sister Emma in Santa Rosa. In this way, an almost psychic link is established between the two Charlies.

Uncle Charlie arrives by steam train, under a large black cloud. Everything is sweetness and light until two men come to interview the family for a national survey. As Charlie falls for one of the men (they are detectives), she begins to doubt her Uncle Charlie is as nice as he seems.

When Charlie realises that her uncle is the Merry Widow murderer, she makes an agreement with the detectives to get charming Uncle Charlie out of town to save distressing her mother too much. Then news comes in that another man is killed and believed to be the murderer – the detectives leave as a result.

Charlie knows her uncle is the real killer, and he knows she knows, so Uncle Charlie twice attempts to kill his niece. In retaliation, Charlie finds a ring – evidence her Uncle Charlie is the killer – and he agrees to leave. As his train begins to move, Uncle Charlie tries to kill her, but he falls out of the train instead.

At the large funeral to commemorate her uncle, Charlie vows to keep her uncle's murders a secret, to protect her mother.

**Subtext:** Small Town Noir. This is a modern-day battle between good and evil, expressed in the duality of Charlie and her Uncle Charlie. Hitch was raised on Victorian literature, like Robert Louis Stevenson's *The Strange Case of Dr Jekyll and Mr Hyde* (1886) and Oscar Wilde's *The Picture of Dorian Gray* (1891), where duality was a major theme. As Charlie grows up (she starts in a dress and ends in a suit) she has to decide whether to protect the world from evil, or to become evil herself. (Uncle Charlie: 'Do you know the world is a foul sty?

Do you know if you ripped the fronts off houses you'd find swine? The world's a hell.')

**Dark Visions:** When Uncle Charlie eludes the two men following him they are small, like ants, to him. To show a connection between Charlie and her uncle, our introduction to them is when they are lying in bed fully-clothed, thinking – Uncle Charlie in Philadelphia, Charlie in Santa Rosa. As the steam train pulls into the station, delivering Uncle Charlie, the incredibly black smoke from the train covers the station in darkness. This is a very light, happy-looking film but it hides a heart of darkness.

**White Noise:** The *Merry Widow Waltz* is heard over the opening credits, and throughout the film, which is appropriate for the Merry Widow murderer. In Hollywood it was convention for every word to be heard but in this film we have overlapping dialogue in the family scenes. When Uncle Charlie makes a speech about old women or the world etc, his voice becomes monotone, which gives him a sinister air.

**Dangerous Ideas:** The Double. Charlie and her Uncle Charlie are twins who share many similar thoughts and feelings – they are two sides of the same coin. As the film begins Charlie wishes for excitement, and Uncle Charlie gives it to her. Santa Rosa is a beautiful town (much like the town in David Lynch's *Blue Velvet*) that lives in an ideal fantasy. It is unreal. Even when Herbie and Joseph talk about murder, it is in a jokey manner because they see it as a game. (Joseph Newton: 'If I wanted to murder you tomorrow, I'd find out if you were alone, walk in, hit you on the head with a lead pipe or a loaded cane...' Herbie Hawkins: 'What would be the fun of that? Where's your planning?')

Charlie's coming of age (with Uncle Charlie as the physical

manifestation of the loss of innocence) means that the town will never be an ideal fantasy again. The horror of life, the pigsty, has been revealed to her. She now knows that real evil is everywhere, that it even exists within those she thinks are closest to her.

**Background:** Hitchcock's mother was ill whilst this film was being made, but he couldn't get to the UK. Hitchcock, normally secretive, began talking about his early life and lots of details made their way into the script. His tenderness towards her probably accounts for the benevolent mother figure, one of the last in his films. The mother is called Emma, the name of Hitchcock's mother. Uncle Charlie's bike accident as a child happened to Hitchcock. Hitchcock refused to drive a car, like Joseph. Ann reads *Ivanhoe*, a book Hitchcock knew by heart as a child. Herbert is mother-dominated and obsessed with murder, perhaps a little like Hitchcock?

**The Verdict:** A perfectly written, acted and directed film which is still fresh and packs a real punch. 5/5

## Double Indemnity (1944)

**Cast:** Fred MacMurray (Walter Neff), Barbara Stanwyck (Phyllis Dietrichson), Edward G Robinson (Barton Keyes), Porter Hall (Mr Jackson), Jean Heather (Lola Dietrichson), Tom Powers (Mr Dietrichson), Byron Barr (Nino Zachetti), Richard Gaines (Edward S Norton), Fortunio Bonanova (Sam Garlopis), John Philliber (Joe Peters)

**Crew:** Director Billy Wilder, Writers Billy Wilder, Raymond Chandler, Novel James M Cain, Producers Buddy G DeSylva (executive), Joseph Sistrom, Composers César Franck (from 'D Minor Symphony'), Miklós Rózsa, Franz Schubert (from 'first movement of 8th symphony'), Cinematographer John F Seitz, Editor Doane Harrison, Costume Designer Edith Head, Art Directors Hans Dreier, Hal Pereira, Sound Stanley Cooley, Walter Oberst, Make-Up Wally Westmore, 107 mins

**Trustee:** Walter Neff

**Traitor:** Phyllis Dietrichson

**Story:** A car races through foggy streets. A man stumbles out of the car, goes up to his office at the Pacific All Risk Insurance Agency and begins dictating a memo to Barton Keyes, dated July 16 1938. This is Walter Neff, insurance agent. He tells his story, obviously in pain from a gunshot wound. We go back in time... Neff dropped in on the Dietrichson house to make sure their car was 'fully covered' although Mrs Dietrichson was only wearing a towel when he said this. The sexual energy between them was heightened when they talked/flirted, making reference to Phyllis Dietrichson's anklet. When they next met it became obvious that Phyllis wanted to insure her husband, kill him, and collect on the money. Neff walked out, but was caught and knew it. Phyllis came to him, kissed him, told Neff about how mean her husband was to her. He turned the murder into a challenge – part of his job as an insurance agent was to work out how to buck the system/crook the house, for the good of the company.

Neff knew that the insurance company paid out double (double indemnity) if certain unusual accidents happened, and worked out a plan. This was how it went down... First they tricked Dietrichson into signing the accident insurance. He broke his leg and was in a cast. But he was going away on business. Neff established his alibi and hid in the back of the Dietrichson car. Dietrichson and Phyllis got into the car and drove to the train station. Phyllis honked the horn to signal for Neff to break Dietrichson's neck. Neff took the crutches, put a bandage on his leg, got aboard the train, went to the observation deck in the end carriage, and jumped off when the train slowed for a corner. Phyllis was waiting. They arranged Dietrichson's body on the tracks and left. They could not see each other for a long time, so that they would not be suspected of being together on this.

The head of the insurance company, Norton, did not want to pay out. He told Phyllis that he thinks her husband had committed suicide, which reduced the pay out. Neff's best friend in the company is investigator Barton Keyes, who has a 'little man' inside him which tells him when there is something wrong with a claim. There was something wrong with the Dietrichson claim, he thought, because why would a man with a broken leg not put in a claim when he had accident insurance? Answer: because he did not know he had accident insurance. In addition, Keyes thought that Phyllis had arranged this with a lover. Keyes could not find the solution because Neff arranged the insurance and was trusted completely.

Neff started seeing Dietrichson's daughter Lola, who was suspicious of her stepmother. Lola told Neff that Phyllis was originally her mother's nurse, and that Phyllis had deliberately left windows open etc, to hasten her mother's death. Then Phyllis had moved in on her father for his money. In addition to this, Lola had split with her hot-headed boyfriend Nino Zachetti, who was now seeing Phyllis.

Taking all this into account, Neff said that, 'We did it so that we could be together, but it's tearing us apart.' Thinking that Phyllis was persuading Zachetti to kill him, Neff tried to frame Zachetti for her murder. He met Phyllis and she shot him. He told her to shoot again, to finish him off, but she could not because she loved him. He shot her point blank. Twice.

We then flash forward to Neff in the office, telling his story,

Keyes listening incredulously in the background. Neff stumbles to the elevator. Keyes lights a match for Neff and they wait for the police.

**Subtext:** There are constant references to the heart, honey, and trains in this complicated and layered script. At the very beginning, the porter explains to Neff that he cannot get insurance and it is 'something about my heart.' This prefigures, Neff's insurance problem – he loses his heart to a femme fatale. And Phyllis' last words to Neff are, 'I'm rotten to the heart.' At one stage Walter Neff says, 'I never knew that murder could smell like honeysuckle.' This is interesting because he calls Phyllis 'Honey' on several occasions. As for trains, in a key (sic) speech Keyes says, 'They've committed a murder and it's not like taking a trolley ride together where they can get off at different stops. They're stuck with each other and they've got to ride all the way to the end of the line and it's a one-way trip and the last stop is the cemetery.' When Neff and Phyllis talk, they says several times that they have to go 'all the way' and 'to the end of the line' as if they know that it is all going to go wrong. The train metaphor is developed further when Neff and Phyllis pretend that Mr Dietrichson died by falling off a train.

Neff has no morals. He knows the system and wants to break it, so his crime is a sort of game for him. He is rebelling against Keyes, who is his father figure and who follows the rules precisely. Keyes treats Neff like a son, and even offers him a position as his assistant. But Keyes is inflexible (to the point that he had his fiancée checked up before their marriage and found dirt on her) and so Neff cannot reason with him. The only way Neff can communicate is by committing a crime and telling his 'father' about it in the dictated memo. At several points, Neff says to Keyes, 'And I love you too,' because Keyes can never say/admit it. Also, Neff is always lighting matches for

Keyes (who thinks it dangerous to carry matches because they can always go off unexpectedly). At the end, with Neff wounded, Keyes lights a match for Neff and we see that perhaps he feels sympathy for the criminal for the first time.

Neff is emulating Keyes by being suspicious of his girl Phyllis (although Neff probably has more reason to be on his guard). This brings up an interesting parallel. Keyes says that he carries a 'little man' around inside him that tells him when something is wrong. Could Neff be carrying a 'little Keyes' around inside him? (Walter Neff: 'Where would the living room be?' Maid: 'In there, but they keep the liquor locked up.' Walter Neff: 'That's okay. I always carry my own key.')

Neff takes over the position of father to Phyllis. Mr Dietrichson is dictatorial to both Phyllis and Lola, treating them like wayward daughters. Neff treats Phyllis the same way, ordering her about, and calling her 'baby.' They even meet by the baby food in Jerry's supermarket. Neff also takes on a fatherly rather than romantic role with Lola after her father's death.

Doubling appears throughout the film. As well as the obvious physical doubling (Neff pretending to be Mr Dietrichson on the train) there is also a psychological doubling – Neff and Zachetti both have relationships with both Phyllis and Lola. And some of these characters are double-crossing each other.

**Dark Visions:** Venetian blinds. Fog.

**White Noise:** Voice-over.

**Dangerous Ideas:** Flashback. Identifying with the murderers. Doubles. Fedora.

**Background:** Billy Wilder had a lot of trouble getting *Double*

*Indemnity* made. First of all, his usual writing partner Charles Brackett was too disgusted by James M Cain's novel to consider working on it. Cain himself was working with Fritz Lang on *Western Union*, so Wilder turned to Raymond Chandler, who had had four tough guy novels published and had never worked in film before. After a week, Chandler submitted his first attempt to Wilder, who said, 'This is shit, Mr Chandler,' and threw the screenplay across the room. They worked together, with Wilder mainly concentrating on plot/structure and Chandler supplying great dialogue. After a little while, the mature, reserved Chandler had problems being in the same room as brash, young, vulgar Wilder – they agreed to collaborate from a distance. The result was a great screenplay, nominated for an Academy Award.

Casting also proved a problem. George Raft did not understand the story because there was no good guy, and other leading actors did not want to be the seedy, immoral lead. Wilder eventually persuaded Fred MacMurray, who was previously known for his lightweight roles. MacMurray experienced a beneficial change of image, like Dick Powell did after he played Philip Marlowe in *Farewell, My Lovely* (1944). *Double Indemnity* also propelled Barbara Stanwyck into the public eye as a domineering femme fatale – she appeared in about a dozen Films Noirs.

Walter Neff was originally named Walter Ness, but when it was found that there was a real insurance salesman in Beverly Hills named Walter Ness, the name was changed to avoid a lawsuit for defamation of character. In fact, Cain had based his novel on a real murder case – in 1927, Albert Snyder was killed by his wife Ruth and Judd Grey to collect Snyder's insurance money.

Filming began on 27 September 1943 and ended 4 weeks later on 24 November. At the end of one day's filming, Billy Wilder could not start his car. He decided to add this incident into the story – after the murder, Neff and Phyllis cannot start their car. An execution scene was shot for the end of the film, where Keyes watches as Neff makes his way to the gas chamber, but it was cut. When Neff says, in his voice-over, 'Suddenly it came over me that everything would go wrong. It sounds crazy, Keyes, but it's true, so help me. I couldn't hear my own footsteps. It was the walk of a dead man, this seems like it was a lead-in to the execution scene.

*Double Indemnity* is the film that launched a million imitators throughout the 1940s and 1950s. Even in recent years, you can see that *Body Heat* (1981) and *The Last Seduction* (1994) are just modern reworkings of the basic premise. It was remade for TV in 1973, directed by Jack Smight (*Harper* [1966]) and written by Steven Bochco (*Hill Street Blues*, *NYPD Blue*), starring Richard Crenna (Neff), Lee J Cobb (Keyes) and Samantha Eggar (Phyllis). Woody Allen also featured a clip from *Double Indemnity* in his Film Noir homage *Manhattan Murder Mystery* (1993).

**The Director:** Billy Wilder, bless him, has co-written and directed some of the bleakest films Hollywood ever made, like *The Lost Weekend* (1945, alcoholic on binge), *Sunset Boulevard* (1950, dead screenwriter tells how an ageing movie star killed him) and *Ace in the Hole* (1951, reporter puts man at risk to prolong story and make himself famous). An émigré writer/director, his rapid dialogue writing style makes him sound like he assimilated to American culture. However, the content shows that he hates hypocrisy, capitalism and selfishness. His films express his moral outrage.

**The Writer:** James M Cain, Raymond Chandler and Dashiell Hammett are considered the holy trinity of the tough guy school of writing. However, whereas Hammett and Chandler portrayed hard men fighting an immoral world, Cain was more interested in exploring the immoral people that made up that world. We follow bad people doing bad things. From *The Postman Always Rings Twice* (1934) to *Mildred Pierce* (1941) and beyond, Cain portrayed women as predatory animals (he used wild cats as a metaphor in *Postman*) who were quite prepared to use their sexual chemistry as a catalyst for controlling men.

**The Photographer:** John F Seitz began his career as a cinematographer in 1916 and worked on 110 movies, including *The Four Horsemen of the Apocalypse* (1921), *This Gun for Hire* (1942) and films for Preston Surges, before *Double Indemnity*. He was a master of the beautiful/dynamic composition made from layers of black. The camera rarely moved, but when it did, it was unobtrusive and completely served the story. His other notable contributions to Film Noir include *The Big Clock* (1948) and *Night Has a Thousand Eyes* (1948).

**The Verdict:** This template for hundreds of Film Noirs is still one of the best. Sparkling dialogue, allusive references, exciting characters, dark photography. 5/5

## *Force of Evil* (1948)

**Cast:** John Garfield (Joe Morse), Thomas Gomez (Leo Morse), Beatrice Pearson (Doris Lowry), Roy Roberts (Ben Tucker), Paul Fix (Bill Ficco), Marie Windsor (Edna Tucker), Howland Chamberlain (Freddie Bauer), Paul McVey (Hobe Wheelock), Georgia Backus (Sylvia Morse), Beau Bridges (Frankie Tucker), Stanley Prager (Wally), Barry Kelley (Egan), Sid Tomack (Two & Two Taylor)

**Crew:** Director Abraham Polonsky, Writers Polonsky, Ira Wolfert, Novel *Tucker's People* by Wolfert, Producer Bob Roberts, Composers David Raksin, Ludwig van Beethoven,

Cinematographer George Barnes, Editors Arthur Seid, Walter Thompson, Art Director Richard Day, Set Decorator Edward G Boyle, Assistant Director Robert Aldrich, Production Manager Joe C Gilpin, Sound Frank Webster, Make-Up Gustaf Norin, 78 mins

**Trustee:** Leo Morse

**Traitor:** Joe Morse

**Story:** Wall Street, New York. A city of ant-like people. Big numbers. The numbers racket. Every day millions of people bet nickels and dimes on a number. If their number comes up, they are lucky. The chances are a million-to-one. 'If you don't get killed, it's a lucky day,' says lawyer Joe Morse. He is the brain for Ben Tucker, the man who wants to run the numbers. Joe tells us that tomorrow, July 4, he is going to make a million. His number is coming up.

The scheme is simple. They are going to fix the number for July 4. People are superstitious, and always bet 776 on July 4. Independence Day. It will be for Joe. This will wipe out all the banks – the independent businessmen who run their own little numbers rackets – who will have to pay off their winners. They will be cleaned out. Tucker will step in, offer to pay off their debts. In return, they have to join Tucker's combination, work under his control.

Joe's lawyer partner, Wheelock, is talking to Hall, trying to legalise the numbers racket, as it is in other countries. Wheelock tells Joe that there is a difference between representing Tucker and doing his business for him. Lawyers are not immune from the law.

Joe is also a brother – he has an older brother called Leo. Leo runs a small numbers bank, thinks himself an honest businessman, doing business for the little people, looking after them. They call the numbers racket policy, because people put their nickels and dimes on the numbers rather than pay off their insurance policies. Joe, knowing that Leo will be wiped out tomorrow, desperately tries to persuade Leo to sell up, but Leo refuses. Leo could have become a lawyer, but he sweated and slaved for Joe, to put him through college. And this is how Leo is repaid. Joe phones the police and tips them off, tells them to raid Leo's bank, to put him out of business, so he will not be wiped out.

After Joe gets the people out of jail, he romances Doris, Leo's secretary, the daughter Leo never had, who quit because she did not want to be a criminal any more. At first she resists, but Joe is so charming, so open (Joe: 'Just to feel guilty – that's a black thing'), so energetic, that she falls for him (Doris: 'To love you is to love something rotten and corrupt within myself').

July 4, the banks go bust, and Tucker moves in. Joe makes Leo the head banker, looking after 13 banks. (Leo does not want it but he has no choice.) Mr Bauer, the bookkeeper, enters the bank, which is full of gangsters. He is afraid and wants to quit. Joe threatens Bauer, politely implying that he will be dead, quitting the bank means he will quit life also. Bauer still wants out, so he squeals to Hall, and is approached by a rival gang.

Mrs Tucker is after Joe's body (and soul?) and tells him in person, because the phones are tapped, and are a direct line to Hall. He picks up the phone and hears the 'click' of the unknown listener. (Joe: 'A man could spend the rest of his life trying to remember what he shouldn't have said.')

Leo's bank is raided again. Ficco, Tucker's former partner back in the prohibition days, wants in on the combination and is willing to use force. Joe wants to save Leo, so he agrees to pay Leo's debts and take over his bank – Joe has made the leap from representing the lawbreaker, to being one.

On his way to collect money from his office, Joe spies Wheelock there, reporting to Hall on the phone. Stuffing his pockets, Joe runs down the deserted Wall Street, a tiny man overwhelmed by the immense structures of capitalism.

Bauer is very afraid, and is leaned on by Ficco's mob. He asks Leo to meet him at a restaurant. Leo is late. As he tries to explain about his heart condition (Leo: 'You're dying while you're breathing') Ficco's mob kidnap Leo, and shoot Bauer.

Joe is drunk at a nightclub, with Doris, when he sees the newspaper – Bauer slain, Leo held hostage – and runs to Tucker. Ficco is with Tucker. They have joined forces, with Ficco as the hard man, the enforcer, the muscle. And Leo? Leo is dead and they have dumped him in the river, on the rocks, by the lighthouse. Enraged, Joe leaves the phone off the hook (for Hall to hear), and spills all the secrets. When Tucker realises, they are thrown into darkness and a gunfight leaves Tucker and Ficco dead.

Joe picks up the phone and tells Hall he'll be down to see the police. With Doris, he goes to the rocks. Down, down, to the bottom of the world. Where he finds his brother's body. Joe: 'If a man's life can be lived so long and come out this way, like rubbish, then something was horrible, and had to be ended one way or another, and I decided to help.'

**Subtext:** Political Noir. The story of how the world works, all nine circles of it. This is the story of a corrupt society, showing how each person must find their own way, make their own decisions. This is the story of one man who finds out the price that has to be paid when all debts are called in.

Both Joe and Leo are crooks. Joe knows and accepts it. He has two aims: to make money, lots of it, and to save his brother Leo. Leo is a crook, but a small-time one. He thinks that he is providing a service to the community because he is small and knows all the people who work for him, and who place bets with him, but he is deluding himself. When Joe realises that Leo is out of his depth, Joe gets Leo a better job so that he makes lots of money. But Leo only realises that he is a crook. Joe responds by trying to get Leo out of the numbers racket altogether. By doing this, Joe is sacrificing his safety because he is breaking the law. At the end, when Leo is dead, Joe decides to help the law. The reason for this is not to be a good person, but to avenge himself against the combination/the numbers racket which helped kill his brother.

Everybody in the movie acts selfishly, for their own good. This includes Doris who works for Leo, and is therefore a criminal. When she quits out of shame (she realises she is a criminal), Joe seduces her with roses (he gives her roses, and there is a rose painted on the wall of the nightclub) and talks of rubies. Eventually, she cracks and turns up at his office to get a job for $100 a week instead of $35. She turns up dressed in black – a sign of her inner corruption by him.

The law is also corrupt, because it is made up of people. The numbers racket only exists because the lawkeepers are paid for not seeing the lawbreakers. There is a scene where Leo is preparing the money to pay off the police. The police know who everybody is. We never see the workings of the law.

For all the power that Joe has, he cannot save his brother. He cannot pay back the debt he owes Leo (who sacrificed his future so that Joe could become a lawyer), about which he feels guilty ('it is a black thing'). For all his striving upwards (to have an office in the clouds), he is forever travelling 'down, down, down... to the bottom of the world.'

After the war, gangsters wanted to assimilate into the free-market economy – to become legit. *Force of Evil* uses the lexicon of big business. What we witness are mergers and takeovers. Polonsky is saying that Corporate America are gangsters. For corporation read 'combination.' It is no accident that Joe has his offices in Wall Street, the heart of capitalist America.

**Dark Visions:** We begin with a high shot of Wall Street skyscrapers and pan down. This is the predominant visual motif – Tucker and Joe walk down a grand staircase at the beginning, and Joe walks down the giant riverside staircase at the end. He only walks up stairs (or elevators) when visiting his brother, or when going to his law office – the only 2 places that offer the hope of redemption.

**White Noise:** Voice-over. Mention must be made of the extraordinary rhythm of the dialogue, which gives you the feeling you are watching Shakespeare in modern dress. The sound level of the dialogue remains the same, no matter how far away the actors, and the images are cut to the rhythm of the sound (or at counterpoint to it). Watching the sequence where Leo arrives at the restaurant and is taken away by the Ficco mob, with the classical music in the background, I'm reminded of a similar sequence in Francis Ford Coppola's *The Godfather* (1972).

**Dangerous Ideas:** Corruption (Joe: 'I wasn't strong enough to resist corruption, but I was strong enough to fight for a piece of it'). Self-delusion. Guilt. Greed. Gangsterism as a metaphor for Capitalism.

**Background:** Polonsky spent as much time as he could on the set of *Body and Soul*, which he wrote, watching how the film was made. Most of all, he watched cameraman James Wong Howe, who used documentary techniques he had learned during the war. When it came to filming *Force of Evil*, Polonsky gave cameraman George Barnes a book on Edward Hopper and told him to emulate it. This can be seen in the way the image is framed, the single source lighting and in the way the camera is often positioned slightly higher than the characters, giving a diagrammatical feel to the story. The first scene they filmed was the end sequence, where Joe goes down, down, to the bottom of the world.

**The Writer/Director:** Born 5 December 1910, Abraham Polonsky was a lawyer, wartime agent for the OSS, professor, novelist and radio writer. He wrote the successful Boxing Noir *Body and Soul* (1947), and joined with its director Robert Rossen and star John Garfield to set up their own independent film company. They made some great movies (*Force of Evil, The Breaking Point, He Ran All the Way*), but the House Un-American Activities Committee made sure that Polonsky was blacklisted. He worked uncredited as a writer on *Odds Against Tomorrow* (1959) but most of his work appeared on TV. His first post-HUAC writing credit was on Don Seigel's *Madigan* (1968), before he wrote/directed *Tell Them Willie Boy Is Here* (1969). He died 26 October 1999.

**The Photographer:** George Barnes (1892–1953) liked to work with black-on-black – there are some scenes which require infra-red to watch them! He probably produced his best work on *Force of Evil*, but he also worked on *Rebecca* (1940), *Spellbound* (1945) and *The File on Thelma Jordon* (1950).

**The Verdict:** It is hard to believe that cash flow could be so exciting, but it is. 5/5

## *The Killing* (1956)

**Cast:** Sterling Hayden (Johnny Clay), Coleen Gray (Fay), Vince Edwards (Val Cannon), Jay C Flippen (Marvin Unger), Ted de Corsica (Randy Kennan), Marie Windsor (Sherry Peatty), Elisha Cook Jr (George Peatty), Joe Sawyer (Mike O'Reilly), James Edwards (Parking Attendant), Timothy Carey

(Nikki Arane), Kola Kwariani (Maurice Oboukhoff), Jay Adler (Leo Tito Vuolo), Dorothy Adams, Herbert Ellis, James Griffith, Cecil Elliott, Joe Turkel (Tiny), Steve Mitchell, Mary Carroll, William 'Billy' Benedict, Charles R. Cane, Robert B Williams

**Crew:** Director Stanley Kubrick, Writers Stanley Kubrick, Jim Thompson (dialogue), Novel *Clean Break* by Lionel White, Producer James B Harris, Associate Producer Alexander Singer, Music Gerald Fried, Cinematographer Lucien Ballard, Editor Betty Steinberg, Art Director Ruth Subotka, Set Decorator Harry Reif, Costume Design Beaumelle, Make-Up Robert Littlefield, Assistant Director Milton Carter, Sound Rex Lipton, 85 mins

**Working Titles:** *Bed of Fear, Day of Violence*

**Trustee:** Johnny Clay

**Traitor:** Society betrays itself

**Story:** Saturday, 3.45pm – Drunk Marvin Unger is at a race-track. He passes an address and time to the barman, and then to a cashier. 2.45pm – Randy, a policeman, meets a man to extend his loan of $3,000, which he promises will be repaid shortly. 7.00pm – Johnny Clay, who has just done a 5-year stretch, tells his girlfriend Fay that he is going for the big one, and he's going to use non-criminals. 6.30pm – Mike O'Reilly, the racetrack bartender, returns home to his sick wife for whom he wants the best. 7.15pm – George Peatty, the race-track cashier, returns home to his mean, sarcastic wife, Sherry. George is a wimp who loves his wife, but she wants a real man, and one with money to boot. When George lets it slip that he'll soon have all the money she could wish for, Sherry wheedles information out of him about the upcoming race-track heist. Cut to Sherry meeting her lover Val Cannon and their plan to take all the money for themselves. Cut to the gang (Johnny, Randy, George, Mike, Marvin) meeting at 8.00pm as arranged and Johnny explaining that he will hire 2 professionals, a shooter and a fighter, to carry out vital parts of the plan, reassuring them that the professionals are on a fixed fee and do not get a share of the estimated $2 million. Marvin put up the money for them. Johnny hears a noise – it's a woman, Sherry, whom he knocks out. George starts whining, Randy hits him, and the whole plan looks compromised. Johnny has a talk with Sherry (Johnny Clay: 'I know you like a book, ya little tramp. You'd sell out your own mother for a piece of fudge. But you're smart with it. Smart enough to know when to sell and when to sit tight. You've got a great big dollar sign where most people have a heart.'), says that he knows she's only interested in money but if she keeps her mouth shut she'll get a bundle. When George and Sherry return home, George wants to call the whole thing off but Sherry persuades him to continue with the plan.

Tuesday, 10.15am – At the Chess Academy, Johnny persuades his friend Maurice Oboukhoff, wrestler and chess master, to start a fight at the racetrack for $2,500. Next he visits professional shooter Nikki Arane. Johnny asks Nikki if he could shoot a horse, Red Lightning, in the 7th race, for $5,000, no questions asked. Nikki agrees. Finally, Johnny gets a motel room from Leo Tito Vuolo, the father of a prison friend. Johnny leaves a package in the motel room.

Saturday 7.30am – George is up early, wide awake, so Sherry suspects the robbery will be today. She pretends Johnny raped her the previous week to make George angry enough to tell her the plan. 5.00am – Johnny tells Marvin to stay away from the track, but Marvin sees Johnny as his son/lover and wants to protect him. 7.00am – Johnny at the airport buys

flight tickets for Fay and himself for 9pm that night. 8.15am –
Johnny goes to the motel, via a florist, and transfers the gun
from his package into the flower box. 8.45am – At the bus
station, Johnny puts the flower box in a locker. 9.20am –
Johnny drops the locker key into Mike's letterbox. 11.15am –
Mike gets ready for work, attends to his sick wife, and collects
the locker key. 11.29am – Mike collects the flower box from
the bus station and gets on the bus to the racetrack. 12.10pm
– Mike in the racetrack locker room, gets changed for work
and puts the flower box in his locker. Nearby, George gets a
small gun and hides it on his person. We follow Mike to his
bar and, as the first race is announced, Marvin turns up drunk.
3.32pm – Randy reports to his superior that his radio is on the
blink. He is on schedule, heading for the racetrack. At the
racetrack, he leans on his car, arms folded, looking up at an
open window, listening to the $7^{th}$ race, the $100,000
Lansdowne Stakes, start. 2.30pm – Maurice leaves his chess
club for the track and, as the $7^{th}$ race starts, he starts a big fight,
distracting the police, and drawing them out of the money
room. As he fights, George opens the security door, Johnny
slips in, and Maurice is dragged away at 4.23pm. 11.40am –
Nikki leaves his farm in his fast car. 12.30pm – Nikki is at the
track car park and, by pretending to have a wooden leg, bribes
the coloured attendant (who has a wooden leg) into letting
him have the spot he wants. At the $7^{th}$ race, the horses are off,
Nikki prepares, shoots Red Lightning, reverses the car, punc-
tures a tyre on a horseshoe, and is shot by the attendant.
4.24pm – Nikki dies. 2.15pm – Johnny is in the city, making
his way to the racetrack. As the $7^{th}$ race is announced, Johnny
sees Marvin drunk, then waits by the security door as Maurice
begins his fight. The guards come through the door and
Johnny is let in by George. In the locker room, he takes the
rifle, puts on a mask and gloves, then takes a sack, knocks on
the money room door, enters, holds 3 men hostage as one of

them fills the sack, puts all the men in the locker room, takes off his outer clothes, stuffs them (and gun) into the sack and throws the sack out the window. As he comes out through the security door a policeman stops Johnny. Marvin bumps him and Johnny knocks him out. Later that evening, Randy, George, Mike and Marvin gather and listen to the radio report and we see that the bag that came out the window, landed at Randy's feet – he took the money and left it in the motel room. Val and a friend crash in, George starts shooting and everybody dies except George, who is badly wounded. 6.25pm – Johnny, with the money in his car, sees George covered with blood as he leaves the hotel so assumes something has gone wrong. Johnny buys the largest suitcase he can find and fills it with the money. Meanwhile, George returns home to find Sherry packing – she betrayed him – and shoots her. George falls dead. At the airport, Fay is waiting for Johnny. Plainclothes police detectives are in the background, as Johnny arrives. At the check-in, Johnny tries to bring the suitcase on the plane as hand luggage, but the assistant will not let him – after an argument, Johnny agrees to check it in. Outside, waiting to board, as the plane taxis, a pet dog runs out, into the path of the luggage truck, which swerves. The suitcase tumbles, flips open and the money is flown into the air, like confetti, by the wind created by the airplane engine. Johnny, in shock, is led out of the airport by Fay. A taxi leaves as they arrive at the front. They hail more taxis but each of them simply goes past. Two policemen slowly walk up to them.

**Subtext:** Docu Heist Noir. Like John Huston's *The Asphalt Jungle* (1950, also starring Sterling Hayden) and other heist movies, this is a meticulous step-by-step, chess-like explanation of how everything that man does is doomed to failure and is self-destructive. Johnny spends the whole of the movie trying to achieve something, but it is all for nothing. It is succinctly summed up by Johnny's last words in the film, 'What's the difference?' We are all food for the worms, so why bother trying to do anything at all?

The fact that this is a crime movie makes this 'moral' ending acceptable to viewers, because the bad men get caught, but the hidden message is that these bad men represent ordinary people – the law enforcer (Randy), the accountant (George), the labourer (Mike), the intellectual/artist (Maurice), the fighter (Nikki), the waster (Marvin) and the gangster (Johnny).

Whilst most Films Noirs talk about betrayal by a colleague or lover, Kubrick shows how people betray themselves – their own nature is against them. No matter what man does, no matter how sophisticated the tools of his craft, he will never progress because of his fatal flaw.

**Dark Visions:** Flashbacks. Kubrick shows the same events from different angles and at different times, giving a refracted, overlapping effect. Lighting. Virtually every shot in this dark film uses single source lighting, or puts layers of intricate shadows over the faces, or plunges the background into black.

**White Noise:** Voice-over. The whole movie is dotted with an authoritative, documentary-type voice telling us times and dates and motivation.

**Dangerous Ideas:** Games. Betting horses, Chess. At the very beginning the voice-over says that Marvin is playing his part in the jigsaw as we see him discard his losing tickets on the floor of the betting office, which is littered with thousands of losing tickets. Later we see the dead bodies of our main characters, littering the floor like those losing tickets. Masks/Disguise. Johnny wears a mask when he commits the robbery, Sherry puts on and takes off her make-up when she's persuading George to do things for her. The Collapse Of Society. Society does not prevent crime or aid the capture of criminals. Fate and its younger brother irony gang up on the criminals. The policeman, a trusted member of society is a criminal. The cashier and barman are both committing a crime for their wives.

**Background:** James B Harris and Stanley Kubrick loved Lionel White's novel *Clean Break* because it presented multiple points of view in fragmented slices of time. Kubrick had already played with flashbacks in *Killer's Kiss* (1955), but here was a good story with solid characters. Harris found out that United Artists were interested in the property for Frank Sinatra, as a follow-on to the successful thriller *Suddenly* (1954), but Sinatra was indecisive about doing it. So Harris asked how much they wanted for the rights – $10,000 – and sent the cheque.

Kubrick hired Noir Fiction novelist Jim Thompson to write the script. Thompson had written more than 10 great noir paperback originals for Lion since 1952 including *The Killer Inside Me* (1952), *Savage Night* (1953), *A Hell of a Woman* (1954), and *After Dark, My Sweet* (1955). The fractured time structure from the novel was copied. Kubrick decided which scenes were to be included and the purpose of each scene, and Thompson went to his room and wrote it up. Thompson added Mike's ailing wife, the wrestler's speech about gangsters & artists ('I often thought that the gangster and the artist are the same in the eyes of the masses. They are admired and hero-worshipped, but there is always present an underlying wish to see them destroyed at the peak of their glory'), and the sadomasochistic relationship between George and Sherry. The novel ends with George shooting Johnny, but there were lots of alternative endings for the movie – one had Johnny go after the money as it swirled about only to get chopped up by the engine propellers. The ending they used owes more than a little to *The Treasure of the Sierra Madre* (1948, d John Huston).

**The Director:** Stanley Kubrick (1928–1999) was a photo journalist for *Look* magazine at the age of 17. His hero was Weegee (real name Arthur Fellig), the news photographer who had the uncanny knack of arriving at crime scenes before the police, hence his nickname. Weegee photos had a surreal air of heightened reality, which Kubrick emulated to a certain extent in *Killer's Kiss* (1955) and *The Killing* (1956). Although Kubrick occasionally used Noir lighting in his other movies, he never did another Film Noir. The closest he came to dealing with Noir themes was in his treatment of obsessive love in *Lolita* (1962), *Barry Lyndon* (1975) and *Eyes Wide Shut* (1999).

**The Writer:** Lionel White (1905–), like Jim Thompson, was a mainstay of the paperback original market in the 1950s who specialised in heist books like *The Snatchers* (1953), *Hostage for a Hood* (1957), *Death Takes the Bus* (1957) and *The Money Trap* (1963). Several of White's novels were adapted by French directors, most notably *Obsession* (1962) by Jean-Luc Godard.

**The Photographer:** Although Lucien Ballard (1908–1988) knocked heads with Kubrick on this movie, he was a name to watch for in the credits because of his subtle black & white photography. He specialised in twilight shots, when the light has a delicate quality. His Films Noirs included *The Lodger* (1944), *Berlin Express* (1948), *Don't Bother to Knock* (1952), *A Kiss Before Dying* (1956) and *Murder by Contract* (1958). At the end of his career he produced some of his most stunning work, on 5 films with maverick director Sam Peckinpah.

**The Verdict:** This has the format of a true crime article turned into a documentary film, but it has added depth because of the great cast of Noir characters and the actors playing them. Every single one of them – dignified Kola Kwariani, slimy Timothy Carey, tough Ted de Corsica, wimp Elisha Cook Jr, vamp Marie Windsor – plays a vital part in bringing it alive. Kubrick's cold, detached, Godlike eye, watches them destroy each other. It's cool. 5/5

## *Touch of Evil* (1958)

**Cast:** Orson Welles (Hank Quinlan), Charlton Heston (Ramon Miguel 'Mike' Vargas), Janet Leigh (Susan Vargas), Joseph Calleia (Pete Menzies), Akim Tamiroff ('Uncle Joe' Grandi), Joanna Cook Moore (Marcia Linnekar), Marlene Dietrich (Tanya), Ray Collins (Adair), Dennis Weaver (Motel Manager), Victor Millan (Manelo Sanchez), Lalo Rios (Risto), Valentin De Vargas (Pancho), Mort Mills (Schwartz), Mercedes McCambridge (Leader of the Gang), Zsa Zsa Gabor (Nightclub Owner), Joseph Cotten (Police Surgeon), Joi Lansing (Blond), Keenan Wynn (Bit Part)

**Crew:** Directors Orson Welles (& Harry Keller), Writers Orson Welles (& Paul Monash, Frankie Coen), Novel *Badge of Evil* by Whit Masterson, Producer Albert Zugsmith, Original Music Henry Mancini, Cinematographers Russell Metty (& Philip H Lathrop, Cliff Stein), Film Editors Edward Curtiss, Aaron Stell, Virgil W Vogel (& Walter Murch on Director's Cut), Art Directors Robert Clatworthy, Alexander Golitzen, Second Unit & Assistant Director Phil Bowles, 112 mins

**Working Title:** *Badge of Evil*

**Trustee:** Pete Menzies

**Traitor:** Hank Quinlan

**Story:** Tick-tock. A bomb is put into the boot of a car in Mexico and it explodes just over the border. A witness is Mike Vargas, recently married to Susan, on their honeymoon – he just caught a druglord called Grandi and is prosecuting him in Mexico City. 'This could be very bad for us,' Vargas says. He decides to stay and help, and sends Susan back to the hotel. Detective Hank Quinlan arrives on the scene with the rest of the force. Linnekar is the dead man. Zita is the dead blonde. Dynamite was used. Motive unknown. Quinlan's leg gives him his hunches as to what is the truth and what is not.

On the way back to her hotel, Susan is waylaid by a handsome Mexican she names Pancho, is surrounded, and taken to see Uncle Joe Grandi. As Uncle Joe looks at himself in the mirror, he tries to threaten her, saying that Vargas is to drop the Grandi case in Mexico City or else, but she is unmoved and says he has been seeing too many gangster movies.

Hank, the Police Chief etc, all go to the strip joint where Linnekar picked up Zita. Outside, a thug throws acid at Vargas, and Vargas chases after him. Inside, the men are attracted to the women, then Hank hears a tune on a distant pianola. Following the sound, he meets his old love Tanya. She does not recognise him – 'You're a mess, honey.'

In her hotel room, Susan is undressing when a bright light is shone into the room from a room opposite. Blinded and annoyed, Susan unscrews the lightbulb in her room and throws it into the room opposite. When Vargas enters, she says she is leaving for the airport but, when Uncle Joe sends her a photo of her and Pancho snapped outside a hotel, Susan says she'll stay in a motel on the American side.

On the way to the motel, they are stopped by Quinlan, who takes Vargas. Pete Menzies drives Susan to the motel. Quinlan forgets his cane, and Pete explains that Hank stopped a bullet for him hence the cane. They are followed by Uncle Joe, but

Pete spots him, arrests him, and drops off Susan at the Mirador Motel.

Quinlan takes Vargas to a construction site, where he suspects the dynamite for the explosion came from, then to Sanchez's apartment. Sanchez, a shoe clerk, is living with Marcia Linnekar, and Quinlan's leg likes him for the hit. Vargas washes his hands and knocks over a shoebox, seeing that it is empty. He leaves to phone Susan, to ensure she is okay, and when he returns finds that Menzies found the dynamite… in the shoebox. When Vargas speaks up, Quinlan is rattled. Quinlan goes off with Uncle Joe, watched by Menzies. Vargas goes off with Schwartz to plot Quinlan's downfall.

Uncle Joe talks Quinlan into setting up Vargas. Uncle Joe says that Susan is being taken care of (Pancho and a juvenile gang take over the motel, persecute Susan, drug her, then leave her naked in a hotel room so that she thinks the worse. Vargas will be so embarrassed by this, he'll have to drop his case against Quinlan.) When Uncle Joe offers Quinlan a drink, Quinlan says he does not drink, then looks down to see that his glass is empty.

Quinlan, now drunk, off the wagon, is found by his best friend Menzies. They talk, about the murder of Quinlan's wife by strangulation ('the smart way to kill'), and the fact that Quinlan never found the killer.

Vargas meets the DA and says that Quinlan planted the dynamite – he shows the DA a document that proves Quinlan has dynamite on his ranch. Quinlan crashes the meeting and says that Vargas is using his position to supply his wife with narcotics.

Vargas goes to the motel, finds Susan missing, races to town, to find Uncle Joe. A hotel in town, Susan half-naked in bed, made to look as though she is on drugs. Quinlan puts on gloves and strangles Uncle Joe. Susan wakes looking up into the dead staring eyes of Uncle Joe Grandi. She screams out the window as Vargas' car drives past.

Vargas rumbles into the Grandi bar, breaks it up, tells them he isn't a cop any more, that he's a husband now. Then he hears that Susan is in jail, accused of murder, and runs to her, embraces her. Menzies takes Vargas aside, shows him Quinlan's cane, which the police found at the murder scene. They agree to illegally trap Quinlan into a confession – Menzies to wear a wire and Vargas to record it.

Menzies talks to Quinlan in a desolate place, but Quinlan realises he is being betrayed, and shoots his best friend Menzies. Crying, he tries to frame Vargas. Seeing the blood on his hands, Quinlan goes down to the river to wash them, and he is shot by a dying Menzies. 'That's the second bullet I've taken for you, partner,' says Quinlan, and falls dead into the river.

Schwartz arrives, telling Vargas that Quinlan was right all along – Sanchez confessed to the bombing. 'He was a great detective.' 'And a lousy cop.'

**Subtext:** Corrupt Cop Noir. Although there are Films Noirs which depict the cop or private eye doing evil because he is out for revenge (*The Big Heat* [1955]), there are also a few where the lawkeeper becomes the lawbreaker (*I Wake Up Screaming* (1941) *The Prowler* (1951), *Rogue Cop* (1954), *Shield for Murder* [1954]). The central question is: Who's the boss: the cop or the law?

*Touch of Evil* is about the decline and fall of Quinlan, as witnessed by Vargas. Quinlan is fascinating because of his moral ambiguity. As Renoir said, 'There is no-one who doesn't have his reasons.' The more human Welles makes Quinlan, the more interesting he becomes. The most complex character in the movie, he is both good and bad. On the plus side, he loves Tanya, he stopped a bullet for Menzies, and he knows from experience who is innocent and who is guilty. On the minus side, he is sometimes both judge, jury and executioner.

The death of Quinlan's wife obviously sent him over the top – he could not find his wife's killer and turned to drink. When Quinlan kills Uncle Joe it has a sexual feel to it, with Susan's groaning and writhing – Quinlan is symbolically killing the man who murdered his wife.

Vargas is transformed by the experience. At first, he is a straight cop, whiter than white, who hates the fact that he has to do the job. 'A soldier doesn't like war.' Then, when Susan is kidnapped he breaks up the Grandi bar and declares, 'I'm no cop now.' (If Vargas had lost Susan, it is almost possible to see him become like Quinlan.) Vargas then uses evil means to trap Quinlan, so he is becoming as bad as Quinlan, and betraying the law. Similarly, Menzies betrays his friend Quinlan, the man to whom he owes his life – Menzies does this because Quinlan betrayed him and the law.

**Dark Visions:** The bravura opening scene starts on a close-up of a bomb, pulls out to see the bomb being put into the boot of a car, and the car driving four blocks to the border, before being blown up. The first cut is on the explosion, which is a quick zoom into it. This is done by skip-framing – alternate frames are cut out (by hand!) to make the zoom quicker. Then there is a hand-held camera sequence as people are running towards the flaming car. All this within the first few minutes!

Other amazing shots include: the Sanchez interrogation scene all done in one take; Schwartz and Vargas in a car going through the town at high speed; the camera swinging up from the ground to a hotel room with a shining torch. The list is endless. There is also a lot of reverse tracking, giving the impression that the people are coming at us all the time. When

Vargas hears his wife is in jail, Welles blurs the picture going out – there are lots of lovely touches like this through the movie.

From the beginning, Quinlan is filmed from below to make his already enormous bulk seem monumental. The only time he seems to weaken is when he hears the pianola music. The first time he looks small is in the scene where Uncle Joe persuades Quinlan to frame Vargas – the pianola music is on in the background, and Quinlan drinks.

As for editing, when people talk, Welles cuts between them so that you see the expressions and reactions of all the participants. He also cuts from one sequence to another, so that everything is happening in parallel – you have no time to breathe.

There are many ironical uses of signs within the movie. For example, as Vargas goes to investigate the explosion the billboard behind him says 'Welcome Stranger.' When Vargas phones Susan from a shop run by a blind woman, behind him can be seen the sign, 'If you are mean enough to rob the blind, help yourself.' After Quinlan has killed Uncle Joe Grandi, he leaves the room and the sign on the door clearly states, 'Stop. Have you left anything?' – Quinlan had forgotten his cane.

**Dangerous Ideas:** Loss of integrity. Betrayal of friends. Woman-in-distress. Race Against time. Nightmare.

**Background:** The Hard-Boiled novel *Badge of Evil* by Whit Masterson (pseudonym for Wade Miller aka Robert Wade and William Miller) sold well and had two hardcover printings when it was published in 1956. Eddie Muhl, head of Universal International, bought the rights and allocated Albert Zugsmith as producer. This self-named King of the Bs, asked Paul Monash to write a script in four weeks. Zugsmith did not care for it, so it got put on a pile.

In December 1956, Muhl suggested Charlton Heston for the lead in *Badge of Evil*. When Heston got the script, Zugsmith asked who he thought should direct. Heston, who was a big star and whose opinion carried weight, said Orson Welles was playing the heavy, so why not ask him? Zugsmith said that because he knew Welles from the shoot of *Man in the Shadow* (1957, d Jack Arnold), he offered Welles a script to direct. Welles asked, 'Which is the worst?' Zugsmith gave him *Badge of Evil* and 2 weeks to rewrite it. Welles took 17 days. Welles used some of the Monash script, put in more scenes from the novel, and then added themes, scenes and characters (Tanya, the night clerk) of his own.

The studio gave Welles Charlton Heston, Janet Leigh and a budget of $895,000. The rest was up to him. Joseph Cotten, Marlene Dietrich, Mercedes McCambridge and Keenan Wynn all agreed to work for union scale wages, without credit, simply to be in a film with Welles. Since Welles was having all his friends in it, Zugsmith got his friend Zsa Zsa Gabor a cameo as well. Welles could not go on location to Mexico so Aldous Huxley suggested that Venice, California would be a suitable location. Welles saw it, liked it and rewrote the end to take place on the bridge.

This was Welles' first Hollywood film in 10 years and he had to show that he was reliable, that he could get the film completed within the budget and on schedule. The studio would have their spies on set, and they would be waiting for him to fail. First day. February 18. 9am. Welles got the first shot at 9.15am, and the second at 9.25am. They were inserts. The studio spies reported back. The studio were happy. Then Welles, assisted by cinematographer Russell Metty (they had worked together on *The Magnificent Ambersons* and *The Stranger*), worked out the Sanchez interrogation scene so that it could be done in one shot. Nothing was shot for hours, as Welles rehearsed the camera going through 3 rooms with breakaway walls, and choreographed the seven speaking parts and extras. The studio were in a sweat. 6.25pm Welles did the whole scene in one shot. 12 pages of script. 2 days ahead of schedule.

To celebrate his return, Welles threw a party for all influential Hollywood moguls. At the time, Welles weighed 270 pounds but to be Quinlan he wanted to be even bigger. He added 60 extra pounds with a false stomach and hump. He acquired a new nose and jowls. He also had a cane because he limped – Quinlan had stopped a bullet for Menzies. Arriving at his party directly from filming, still wearing his grotesque make-up and clothes, all the bigwigs shook his hand vigorously and said he never looked so good!

Janet Leigh did the whole film with a broken left arm – it was in a cast most of the time, heavily disguised, covered or not shown. She was not the only injured one. Whilst filming in Venice, Welles fell into a canal and hurt his ankle so badly he really did need the cane. The injuries were extensive. His face was bruised, but that was covered with make-up. He sprained his wrist, ankle and knee. When not in front of the camera, Welles sported an arm-sling and splint.

On March 14, for the long opening sequence – a bravura crane shot over four blocks – they were up all night rehearsing and filming. Each time something would go wrong, usually the guard who had to say his lines at the end. Eventually, the sun was about to rise, and on the last shot they got it.

The last scene was filmed on the last day of the shoot, on April 2, then the editing and Welles' problems began. When Eddie Muhl and the executives saw a rough cut on July 22, they did not like it so Ernest Nims, a Universal executive with an editing background – he had worked with Welles on *The Stranger* – was brought in to edit the film with Welles. About half of Welles' 40 suggestions were put in by Nims. Universal decided that, in the interest of clarity, extra scenes were to be shot. They got Harry Keller, then a TV director to duplicate Welles' style as best they could. Welles saw the Keller footage edited into the film and sent a 70-page document of comments. Again, about half of them were included. The main thrust of Welles' argument was regarding style. Welles wanted a fragmented style, with more jumping between scenes/locations, whereas the studio wanted a smooth, linear continuity as was normal during that period. Welles' purpose in using this style was to create an atmosphere of nightmare and strangeness, whereas the new scenes and studio editing made it seem more normal.

Upon its release in February 1958, there was no press showing, and *Touch of Evil* played as the B-picture on a double bill. Ironically, Universal released Welles' initial short version, and when the 'long' version with Keller's footage was found in 1981, many proclaimed this as the long-lost 'uncut' Welles version. In 1999, Walter Murch released a reconstructed Director's Cut based on Welles' 70 page memo.

**The Director:** Orson Welles (1915–1985) is a major contributor to Film Noir cinema both in terms of visuals (deep focus, sweeping camera movement, extreme angles, expressionist lighting), sounds (voice-overs, overlapping dialogue), storytelling devices (flashbacks, multiple viewpoints) and of themes (betrayal of lovers & friends, jealousy, corruption of power).

**The Photographer:** Russell Metty (1906–1978) contributed to many Films Noirs, including *Ride the Pink Horse* (1947), *Kiss the Blood Off My Hands* (1948).

**The Verdict:** Since its release *Touch of Evil* has remained a firm favourite of Film Noir enthusiasts and has recently been renovated to classic status by 'respectable' critics, which is the least it deserves. Great from top to bottom, and from beginning to end, this has great performances from Welles and Calleia, and some of Welles' most assured direction. 5/5

## *Vertigo* (1958)

**Cast:** James Stewart (John 'Scottie' Ferguson), Kim Novak (Madeleine Elster/Judy Barton), Barbara Bel Geddes (Marjorie 'Midge' Wood), Tom Helmore (Gavin Elster), Henry Jones (Coroner), Raymond Bailey (Scottie's Doctor), Ellen Corby (Manageress of McKittrick Hotel), Konstantin Shayne (Pop Leibel), Lee Patrick (Older Mistaken Identification)

**Crew:** Director Alfred Hitchcock, Screenplay Samuel A Taylor, Alec Coppel, Novel *The Living and the Dead* by Pierre Boileau, Thomas Narcejac, Producer Alfred Hitchcock, Associate Producer Herbert Coleman, Original Music Bernard Herrmann, Cinematographer Robert Burks, Film Editing George Tomasini, Art Direction Henry Bumstead, Hal Pereira, Assistant Director Daniel McCauley, Special Effects John P Fulton, Title Designer Saul Bass, 120 mins

**Trustee:** Scottie Ferguson

**Traitor:** Madeleine Elster/Judy Barton

**Story:** Detective Scottie is chasing a criminal across the rooftops of San Francisco when he discovers he has vertigo – a fear of heights – and causes the death of a policeman. Recovering and retired – he has independent means – he relaxes with his best friend Midge, a college friend who loves him, although Scottie doesn't realise it. Another old college friend, Gavin Elster, wants Scottie to follow his wife Madeleine because he believes her to be possessed by the spirit of her grandmother, Carlotta Valdez, who committed suicide.

Scottie follows Madeleine, and falls in love with her. When she throws herself into the bay, he saves her. They love each other, but Madeleine must go to a church tower, where she falls and dies. Scottie is heartbroken, his vertigo stopped him from saving her, and his mind goes. Midge helps him recover, but she knows Scottie still loves Madeleine. Released, everything and everyone Scottie sees reminds him of Her, and then he sees her double, Judy Barton. Following her, he begins to change her into the Madeleine he wants. (We know that she is the same woman, that she was used by Elster to imitate his wife, that Elster knew Scottie had vertigo, and that it was Elster's wife who fell from the tower, not Judy. Also, we know that Judy fell in love with Scottie for real. It is only a matter of time before Scottie finds this out.) When Judy wears Carlotta Valdez's necklace, Scottie knows and takes her back to the church tower. In his anger, he forces her to the top, overcoming his vertigo and, as they profess their love for each other, Judy cowers away from a shadow and falls to her death, leaving Scottie wrought with guilt and woe.

**Subtext:** Obsession Noir. This is one of the great stories of obsession, a recurring theme in Hitchcock's work. It shows how an intelligent man can make the same mistakes over and over again, reliving it in his mind. How can he trust other people, when he cannot even trust himself? However, the opportunity arises for him to make his dream come true once more – he cannot resist living his dream again. And then, for the third time in his life, he makes a big mistake.

The key to this extraordinary work is the visit to the Sequoias. We see a cross-section of an old tree trunk, and history is shown repeating itself through wars and treaties. And the name of the trees translates as 'Always green, everlasting.' This explains why, when we first see Madeleine, and then later Judy Barton, she is wearing green, and in profile. Madeleine even drives a green car. Also, the green light (from the neon light) bathes Judy when she is transformed back into Madeleine. Carlotta becomes Madeleine becomes Judy – they are objects of love reincarnated, remade, over and over. They are everlasting, because Scottie will always love her, even after death. It's a romantic, gothic idea played out in bright sunshine.

**Dark Visions:** Where to begin? When Scottie meets Elster, the framing is symmetrical, their body language is the same then changes as they talk, Scottie starting high (in power position) and Elster low, and ending up reversed as Scottie is persuaded by Elster's argument. At Ernie's, we pan from Scottie to room, the music kicks in, and we track in slowly to Madeleine: she is wearing green, and is seen from the side (aloof). Madeleine is seen in mirrors several times, as is Judy. It is all about dressing and undressing (Scottie undresses Madeleine when he saves her from the Bay, and then proceeds to dress Judy as Madeleine – the undressing allowed him to be precise in this matter). The first half is seen from Scottie's point of view, and the second from Judy's.

**Dangerous Ideas:** Doubles (Madeleine Elster thinks she's Carlotta Valdes but she's really Judy Barton, Judy makes the crack that Scottie can't kiss her because she's got her face on, Midge paints herself as Carlotta Valdes, Scottie kills two people through his vertigo, and the love of his life dies twice).

**The Verdict:** A classic Film Noir although it is rarely referenced as such. The Scottie is a private eye who falls for a femme fatale. He then finds/loses her. At the end, Scottie is completely broken. Pessimistic? You bet. Moody? Right. Is Scottie obsessed? Yep. Wordless for most of its length, it says more as a result. The film gains resonance from repeated viewing. 5/5

# Filmography

This is the scenario… You are sitting down with a copy of the TV listings, trying to work out whether or not to record a film on video. Is it, or is it not a Film Noir? A decision has to be made. May I suggest that perusing the list below will help you make that decision.

There is a short list of Pre-Noir Period films and films of the French Poetic Realists. Then there is a list of 647 Film Noirs from the classic period (1940–1960) which include short credits and story information. This is a compilation of all the Films Noirs referenced in other books, so it is longer than any other I have seen, and it has been extended considerably for this second edition. Next there are other American Noirs from 1961 to 1975 listed alphabetically, and then Neo-Noirs from 1976 to 1992 listed by year. Finally, there are short lists of Films Noirs from around the world.

For this edition I have added a lot of hard-boiled poverty row films from the 1950s and have expanded the list to include films with exceptional noir photography in other genres (Horror, Western, Gothic) and social drama films with noir situations. You can find out more information about the film directors and some of the other film movements by reading the Pocket Essentials on *Alfred Hitchcock*, *Billy Wilder*, *Orson Welles*, *Stanley Kubrick*, *German Expressionist Film* and *French New Wave*.

Key to credits: d = director, sc = screenplay, ad = adaptation, st = story, n = novel, pl = play, ar = article, ph = photography, c = cast

# American Pre-Noir

*Underworld* (1927) d Josef von Sternberg
*The Racket* (1928) d Lewis Milestone
*Thunderbolt* (1929) d Josef von Sternberg
*The Big Gamble* (1931) d Fred Noble
*City Streets* (1931) d Rouben Mamoulian
*The Maltese Falcon* (1931) d Roy Del Ruth
*The Secret Six* (1931) d George W Hill
*The Beast of the City* (1932) d Charles Brabin
*I Am a Fugitive from a Chain Gang* (1932) d Mervyn LeRoy
*Payment Deferred* (1932) d Lothar Mendes
*Two Seconds* (1932) d Mervyn LeRoy
*Advice to the Lovelorn* (1933) d Alfred L Werker
*Blood Money* (1933) d Rowland Brown
*Crime Without Passion* (1934) d Ben Hecht, Charles MacArthur
*Midnight* (1934) d Chester Erskine
*Bordertown* (1935) d Archie Mayo
*The Glass Key* (1935) d Frank Tuttle
*The Scoundrel* (1935) d Ben Hecht, Charles MacArthur
*Bullets or Ballots* (1936) d William Keighley
*Fury* (1936) d Fritz Lang
*The Petrified Forest* (1936) d Archie Mayo
*You Only Live Once* (1937) d Fritz Lang
*You and Me* (1938) d Fritz Lang
*Blind Alley* (1939) d Charles Vidor
*Let Us Live* (1939) d John Brahm
*Rio* (1939) d John Brahm

# German Expressionists

*The Cabinet of Dr Caligari* (1920) d Robert Wiene
*Dr Mabuse: The Gambler* (1922) d Fritz Lang
*Sunrise* (1927) d F W Murneau

*M* (1931) d Fritz Lang
*The Testament of Dr Mabuse* (1933) d Fritz Lang

## French Poetic Realists

*La Bête Humaine* (1938) d Jean Renoir
*La Chienne* (1931) d Jean Renoir
*Le Corbeau* (1943) d Henri-Georges Clouzot
*Le Dernier Tournant* (1939) d Pierre Chenal
*Le Jour Se Lève* (1939) d Marcel Carné
*Pépé le Moko* (1936) d Julien Duvivier
*Pièges* (1939) d Robert Siodmak
*Le Quai des Brumes* (1938) d Marcel Carné

## Film Noir (1940–1960)

*711 Ocean Drive* (1950) d Joseph M Newman, sc Richard English, Francis Swan, ph Franz Planer, c Edmond O'Brien. Man uses technical knowledge to take over gambling syndicate.

*99 River Street* (1953) d Phil Karlson, sc Robert Smith, st George Zuckerman, ph Franz Planer, c John Payne. Ex-boxer framed for wife's murder by her criminal lover.

*Abandoned* (1949, *Abandoned Woman*) d Joseph M Newman, sc ar Irwin Gielgud (& William Bowers), ph William Daniels (& David S Horsley), c Dennis O'Keefe, Gale Storm, Jeff Chandler, Raymond Burr, Mike Mazurki. Melodramatic baby-stealing story, great photography.

*Accomplice* (1946) d Walter Colmes sc Irving Elman, Frank Gruber, n *Simon Lash, Private Detective* Frank Gruber, c Richard Arlen. Hardboiled fun.

*The Accused* (1948) d William Dieterle, sc Ketti Frings, n *Be Still, My Love* June Truesdell, ph Milton Krasner, c Loretta Young, Robert Cummings. Nightmare Noir. Psychology professor accidentally kills student who comes on to her.

*Accused of Murder* (1956) d Joseph Kane, sc W R Burnett, Bob Williams, n *Vanity Row* Burnett, c David Brian. Adaptation of Burnett's excellent novel.

*Ace in the Hole* (1951, *The Big Carnival*) d Billy Wilder, sc Billy Wilder, Lesser Samuels, Walter Newman, ph Charles B Lang, c Kirk Douglas. Cynical black satire on newspaperman. 5/5

*Act of Violence* (1949) d Fred Zinnemann, sc Robert L Richards, st Collier Young, ph Robert Surtees, c Van Heflin, Robert Ryan, Janet Leigh. Wartime vet hunted from light into darkness.

*Affair in Havana* (1957) d Laslo Benedek, sc Burton Lane, Maurice Zimm, st Janet Green, ph Allen Stensvold, c John Cassavetes, Raymond Burr. Deadly love affair.

*Affair in Reno* (1957) d R G Springsteen, sc John K Butler, s Gerald Drayson Adams, c John Lund, Doris Singleton. Female detective falls for PR man.

*Affair in Trinidad* (1952) d Vincent Sherman, sc Oscar Saul, James Gunn, st Virginia Van Upp, Berne Giler, ph Joseph Walker, c Rita Hayworth, Glenn Ford. Man suspects/loves widow of brother.

*Alias Nick Beal* (1949, *The Contact Man*) d John Farrow, sc Jonathan Latimer, s Mindret Lord, c Ray Milland, Thomas Mitchell, Audrey Totter. A man rises to power but loses his morality. Political Noir.

*All My Sons* (1948) d Irving Reis, sc Chester Erskine, pl Arthur Miller, ph Russell Metty, c Edward G Robinson, Burt Lancaster. Family melodrama.

*All the King's Men* (1949) d sc Robert Rossen, n Robert Penn Warren, ph Gert Anderson, c Broderick Crawford. Political noir à la *Citizen Kane*. 5/5

*The Amazing Mr X* (1948, *The Spiritualist*) d Bernard Vorhaus, sc Muriel Roy Bolton, Ian McLellan Hunter, st Crane Wilbur, ph John Alton, c Turhan Bey, Lynn Bari. A woman cannot forget her dead husband and gets sucked into a dream world.

*Among the Living* (1941) d Stuart Heisler, sc Lester Cole, Garrett Fort, st Cole, Brian Marlow, ph Theodor Sparkuhl, c Albert Dekker. Man hunts insane brother/killer. 3/5

*Angel Face* (1953) d Otto Preminger, sc Frank Nugent, Oscar Millard, st Charles Erskine, ph Harry Stradling, c Robert Mitchum, Jean Simmons. Doomed love for femme fatale.

*Angels Over Broadway* (1940) d Ben Hecht, Lee Garmes, sc Hecht, ph Lee Garmes, c Douglas Fairbanks Jr, Rita Hayworth.

*Another Man's Poison* (1952) d Irving Raper, sc Val Guest, pl Leslie Sands, ph Robert Krasker, c Bette Davis. Writer/killer Davis blackmailed by criminal on run.

*Apology for Murder* (1945) d Sam Newfield, sc s Fred Myton, c Ann Savage. Unabashed rip-off of *Double Indemnity*.

*Appointment with a Shadow* (1958) d Richard Carlson, sc Alec Coppel, Norman Jolley, st Hugh Pentecost, ph William E Snyder. Nosey reporter becomes killer's target.

*Appointment with Danger* (1951) d Lewis Allen, sc Richard Breen, Warren Duff, ph John F Seitz, c Alan Ladd. PO investigator versus robbers.

*Arch of Triumph* (1948) d Lewis Milestone, sc Harry Brown and Erich Maria Remarque, n Remarque, ph Russell Metty, c Ingrid Bergman, Charles Boyer, Charles Laughton. Dire story of unsavoury refugees roaming Europe pre World War Two.

*Armoured Car Robbery* (1950) d Richard Fleischer, sc Earl Fellows, Gerald Drayson Adams, st Robert Angus, Robert Leeds, ph Guy Roe, c Charles McGraw. Caper with double-crossing mastermind. Stunning photography.

*The Arnelo Affair* (1947) d sc Arch Oboler, st Jane Burr, ph Charles Salerno, c John Hodiak. Woman's psychological melodrama.

*The Asphalt Jungle* (1950) d John Huston, sc Ben Maddow, Huston, n W R Burnett, ph Harold Rosson, c Sterling Hayden. Heist Noir. Great caper-goes-wrong movie with virtuoso images/script/performances. 5/5

*Assigned to Danger* (1948) d Budd Boetticher, sc Eugene Ling, s Robert E Kent, c Gene Raymond. Insurance investigator goes undercover as Doctor to crack payroll robbery case.

*Baby Face Nelson* (1957) d Don Seigel, sc Daniel Mainwaring, st Robert Adler, ph Hal Mohr, c Mickey Rooney. Tough, unsentimental doomed gangster flick.

*Backfire* (1950) d Vincent Sherman, sc Larry Marcus, Ivan Goff, Ben Roberts, st Marcus, ph Carl Guthrie, c Virginia Mayo. War vet hunts for missing friend. Into the darkness.

*Backlash* (1947) d Eugene Forde, sc Irving Elman, ph Benjamin Kline, c Jean Rogers. Lawyer frames wife for his own murder.

*Bait* (1954) d Hugo Haas, sc Samuel W Taylor, Haas, ph Eddie Fitzgerald, c Cleo Moore, Haas, John Agar.

*The Beat Generation* (1959) d Charles Haas, sc Richard Matheson, Lewis Meltzer, ph Walter H Castle, c Steve Cochran, Mamie Van Doren. Duality of cop/criminal.

*Behind Green Lights* (1946) d Otto Brower, sc Charles G Booth, W Scott Darling, ph Joe MacDonald, c Carole Landis, William Gargan. Cop investigates political murder.

*Behind Locked Doors* (1948) d Budd Boetticher, sc Martin Wald, Eugene Ling, st Wald, ph Guy Roe. Reporter goes inside mental hospital to find missing judge.

*Behind the High Wall* (1956) d Abner Biberman, sc Harold Jack Bloom, s Richard K Polimer, Wallace Sullivan, c Tom Tully, Sylvia Sidney. A prison breakout, a corrupt warden and an innocent inmate.

*Below the Deadline* (1946) d William Beaudine, sc Harvey Gates, Forrest Judd, s Ivan Tors, ph Harry Neumann, c Warren Douglas, Ramsay Ames. A war veteran takes over his dead brother's gangster business.

*Berlin Express* (1948) d Jacques Tourneur, sc Harold Medford, st Curt Siodmak, ph Lucien Ballard. Post-war Germany setting for pessimistic Nazi thriller. The city brought alive by photography.

*Betrayal from the East* (1945) d William A Berke, sc Kenneth Gamet, Aubrey Wisberg, n Alan Hynd, ph Russell Metty, c Lee Tracy, Nancy Kelly. Carnival barker becomes double agent.

*Between Midnight and Dawn* (1950) d Gordon Douglas, sc Eugene Ling, st Gerald Drayson Adams, Leo Katcher, ph George E Diskant, c Mark Stevens, Edmond O'Brien. Two cops hunt killer.

*Beware, My Lovely* (1952) d Harry Horner, sc st pl Mel Dinelli, ph George E Diskant, c Ida Lupino, Robert Ryan. Widow and handyman distrust each other in psychological thriller.

*Bewitched* (1945) d sc st Arch Oboler, ph Charles Salerno. Schizophrenic woman kills fiancé on eve of wedding.

*Beyond a Reasonable Doubt* (1956) d Fritz Lang, sc Douglas Morrow, ph William Snyder, c Dana Andrews, Joan Fontaine. To discredit capital punishment, novelist takes blame for murder. 4/5

*Beyond the Forest* (1949) d King Vidor, sc Lenore Coffee, n Stuart Engstrand, ph Robert Burks, c Bette Davis, Joseph Cotten. Small town melodrama.

*The Big Bluff* (1955) d W Lee Wilder, sc Fred Freiberger, st Mindret Lord, ph Gordin Avil. Man marries dying woman for money, then she recovers, so he plans murder. *The Glass Alibi* remake by same team.

*The Big Clock* (1948) d John Farrow, sc Jonathan Latimer, ad Harold Goldman, n Kenneth Fearing, ph John F Seitz, c Ray Milland, Charles Laughton. Business noir set in offices of crime magazine. 4/5

*The Big Combo* (1955) d Joseph H Lewis, sc Philip Yordan, ph

John Alton, c Cornel Wilde, Richard Conte. Savage cop hunts sophisticated villain. Fetishistic sex and sadistic violence. 5/5

*The Big Heat* (1953) d Fritz Lang, sc Sydney Boehm, n William P McGivern, ph Charles B Lang, c Glenn Ford, Gloria Grahame, Lee Marvin. Cop goes off rails in sadistic/violent revenge thriller. 4/5

*The Big Knife* (1955) d Robert Aldrich, sc James Poe, pl Clifford Odets, ph Ernest Laszlo, c Jack Palance, Ida Lupino. Hollywood noir.

*The Big Night* (1951) d Joseph Losey, sc Stanley Ellin, Losey, n *Dreadful Summit* Ellin, ph Hal Mohr. Teenager's rites of passage in noir world.

*The Big Sleep* (1946) d Howard Hawks, sc William Faulkner, Leigh Brackett, Jules Furthman, n Raymond Chandler, ph Sid Hickox, c Humphrey Bogart, Lauren Bacall. Philip Marlowe investigates blackmail, and wisecracks through LA underworld. Also available as Director's cut. 5/5

*The Big Steal* (1949) d Don Seigel, sc Geoffrey Homes (Daniel Mainwaring), Gerald Drayson Adams, s *The Road to Carmichaels* Richard Wormser, ph Harry J Wild, c Robert Mitchum, Jane Greer, William Bendix. Top notch money chase. 5/5

*Big Town* (1947) d William C Thomas, sc Daniel Mainwaring (Geoffrey Homes), Maxwell Shane, st Mainwaring (Homes), ph Fred Jackman Jr, c Phillip Reed. New editor wants yellow journalism to build circulation and ruins people.

*Black Angel* (1946) d Roy William Neill, sc Roy Chanslor, n Cornell Woolrich, ph Paul Ivano, c Dan Duryea. Woman hunts killer of femme fatale to save accused husband. Great photography.

*The Black Hand* (1950) d Richard Thorpe, sc Luther Davis, st Leo Townsend, ph Paul C Vogel, c Gene Kelly. Son seeks revenge when Mafia kills father.

*Blackmail* (1947) d Lesley Selander, sc Royal K Cole, Albert DeMond, st Robert Leslie Bellem, ph Reggie Lanning, c William Marshall. PI Dan Turner takes a case.

*Black Tuesday* (1954) d Hugo Fregonese, sc st Sydney Boehm, ph Stanley Cortez, c Edward G Robinson. Gangster escapes on day of execution.

*Black Widow* (1954) d sc Nunnally Johnson, s Patrick Quentin, ph Charles G Clarke, c Ginger Rogers, Van Heflin, Gene Tierney, George Raft. Bitchy actress accused of murder.

*Blind Spot* (1947) d Robert Gordon, sc Martin Goldsmith, st Barry Perowne, ph George B Meehan. Mystery writer accused of publisher's murder.

*Blonde Alibi* (1946) d Will Jason, sc George Bricker, s Gordon Kahn, ph Maury Gertsman, c Tom Neal, Martha O'Driscoll.

*Blonde Ice* (1948) d Jack Bernhard, sc Kenneth Gamet, Raymond Schrock, Dick Irving Hyland, Edgar G Ulmer, n *Once Too Often* Whitman Chambers, ph George Robinson, c Robert Paige, Leslie Brooks. Society reporter marries wealthy men, who then die.

*The Blue Dahlia* (1946) d George Marshall, sc Raymond Chandler, ph Lionel Lindon, c Alan Ladd, Veronica Lake. War vet accused of murdering unfaithful wife. 3/5

*The Blue Gardenia* (1953) d Fritz Lang, sc Charles Hoffman, st Vera Caspary, ph Nicholas Musuraca, c Anne Baxter, Richard Conte. Newspaperman helps girl who thinks she is a killer. 2/5

*Bluebeard* (1944) d Edgar G Ulmer, sc Pierre Gendron, st Arnold Phillips, Werner H Furst, ph Jockey A Feindell, c John Carradine. Sympathetic murderer must kill women.

*A Blueprint for Murder* (1953) d sc Andrew L Stone, ph Leo Tover, c Joseph Cotten. Man tries to prove sister-in-law is poisoner.

*Blues in the Night* (1941) d Anatole Litvak, sc Robert Rossen, pl Edwin Gilbert, ph Ernest Haller. Tough life of small swing band in noir milieu.

*Body and Soul* (1947) d Robert Rossen, sc Abraham Polonsky, ph James Wong Howe, c John Garfield. Socialist noir boxing story full of grit. 5/5

*Bodyguard* (1948) d Richard Fleischer, sc Fred Niblo Sr, Harry Essex, st George W George, Robert B Altman, ph Robert de Grasse, c Lawrence Tierney. Bodyguard is ex-Detective looking for evidence after murder frame.

*The Bonnie Parker Story* (1956) d William Whitney, sc Stanley Shpetner, ph Jack Marta, c Dorothy Provine, Jack Hogan. Okay retelling of the folk hero robbers, with stylish performance by Provine. 3/5

*Boomerang!* (1947) d Elia Kazan, sc Richard Murphy, ar Anthony Abbott, ph Norbert Brodine, c Dana Andrews. Small town noir as political/social pressure makes innocent man scapegoat for murder.

*Border Incident* (1949) d Anthony Mann, sc John C Higgins, st Higgins, George Zuckerman, ph John Alton, c Ricardo Montalban. Authentic illegal immigration milieu for violent police thriller. 4/5

*Borderline* (1950) d William A Seiter, sc s Devery Freeman, ph Lucien N Andriot, c Fred MacMurray, Claire Trevor, Raymond Burr. Two cops go undercover to catch drug trafficker. Comedy Noir.

*Born to be Bad* (1950) d Nicholas Ray, sc Edith Sommer, ad Charles Schnee, n *All Kneeling* Ann Parish, ph Nicholas Musuraca, c Joan Fontaine, Robert Ryan. Femme fatale married to money, also wants novelist.

*Born to Kill* (1947) d Robert Wise, sc Eve Greene, Richard Macaulay, n *Deadlier than the Male* James Gunn, ph Robert de Grasse, c Claire Trevor, Lawrence Tierney. Selfish woman loves killer. 4/5

*The Boss* (1956) d Byron Haskin, sc Dalton Trumbo, ph Hal Mohr, c John Payne. Sociological Noir.

*The Brasher Doubloon* (1947) d John Brahm, sc Dorothy Hannah, ad Dorothy Bennett, Leonard Praskins, n *The High Window* Raymond Chandler, ph Lloyd Ahern, c George Montgomery. Philip Marlowe on hunt for stolen coins.

*The Breaking Point* (1950) d Michael Curtiz, sc Ranald MacDougall, n *To Have and Have Not* Ernest Hemingway, ph Ted McCord, c John Garfield, Patricia Neal. Charter-boat owner struggles to survive and ends up smuggling. Great, depressing. Better than Bogart/Bacall offering. 5/5

*The Bribe* (1949) d Robert Z Leonard, sc Marguerite Roberts, st Frederick Nebel, ph Joseph Ruttenberg, c Robert Taylor, Ava Gardner. Femme fatale interferes with Federal agent stopping smugglers.

*The Brothers Rico* (1957) d Phil Karlson, sc Lewis Meltzer, Ben Perry, n Georges Simenon, ph Burnett Guffey, c Richard Conte. Reformed criminal Eddie Rico hunts down his brothers to save them from mobsters.

*Brute Force* (1947) d Jules Dassin, sc Richard Brooks, st Robert Patterson, ph William Daniels, c Burt Lancaster, Hume Cronyn. Powerful prison noir tells story of five inmates, a sadistic guard and a riot. 4/5

*A Bullet for Joey* (1955) d Lewis Allen, sc James Benson Nablo, Geoffrey Homes (Daniel Mainwaring), A I Bezzerides, c Edward G Robinson, George Raft.

*The Burglar* (1957) d Paul Wendkos, sc n David Goodis, ph Don Malkames, c Dan Duryea, Jayne Mansfield. Stylish movie about a burglar, his gal, his gang and crooked cop tailing them. 4/5

*Bury Me Dead* (1947) d Bernard Vorhaus, sc Karen DeWolf, Dwight V Babcock, radio pl Irene Winston, ph John Alton, c Cathy O'Donnell. Woman spoils womanising husband's plans by turning up to her own funeral.

*C-Man* (1949) d Joseph Lerner, sc Bernard Giler, ph Gerald Hirschfeld, c Dean Jagger. Docu Noir following customs agent hunting jewel thieves.

*Caged* (1950) d John Cromwell, sc Virginia Kellogg, Bernard C Schoenfeld, ph Carl Guthrie, c Eleanor Parker, Agnes Moorehead. Pithy prison noir of innocent woman becoming tough behind bars.

*Calcutta* (1947) d John Farrow, sc Seton I Miller, ph John F Seitz, c Alan Ladd. Pilot in India seeks friend's killer.

*Call Northside 777* (1948) d Henry Hathaway, sc Jerome Cady, Jay Dratler, ad Leonard Hoffman, Quentin Reynolds, ar James P McGuire, ph Joe MacDonald, c James Stewart, Richard Conte. Docu Noir follows reporter proving man innocent of murder 12 years earlier. 3/5

*Calling Homicide* (1956) d sc Edward Bernds, ph Harry Neumann, c Bill Elliott. Another hard boiled case for police detective Andy Doyle.

*Canon City* (1948) d sc Crane Wilbur, ph John Alton, c Scott Brady. Prison Noir.

*Captive City* (1952) d Robert Wise, sc Karl Kamb, Alvin M Josephy Jr, st Josephy, ph Lee Garmes, c John Forsythe. Editor discovers town owned by mob.

*The Capture* (1950) d John Sturges, sc Niven Busch, ph Edward Cronjager, c Lew Ayres, Teresa Wright. Mexican Noir of hunter becoming hunted.

*Cargo to Capetown* (1950) d Earl McEvoy, sc Lionel Houser, ph Charles Lawton Jr, c Broderick Crawford, John Ireland.

*Cat People* (1942) d Jacques Tourneur, sc DeWitt Bodeen, ph Nicholas Musuraca, c Simone Simon. Great and subtle psychological horror film with many Noir touches. Horror Noir. 5/5

*Caught* (1949) d Max Ophüls, sc Arthur Laurents, n *Wild Calendar* Libbie Block, ph Lee Garmes, c Robert Ryan, James Mason, Barbara Bel Geddes. Anti-capitalist Noir shows woman marry for money then discover values.

*Cause for Alarm* (1951) d Tay Garnett, sc Mel Dinelli, Tom Lewis, st Larry Marcus, ph Joseph Ruttenberg, c Loretta Young. Nightmare Noir of desperate woman trying to prevent being framed by husband for his murder.

*Chain of Evidence* (1957) d Paul Landres, sc Elwood Ullman, ph Harry Neumann, c Bill Elliott. Another case for Lt. Andy Doyle.

*Champion* (1949) d Mark Robson, sc Carl Foreman, st Ring Lardner, ph Franz Planer, c Kirk Douglas. Boxing Noir of fighter smashing way to top. Bleak. 5/5

*The Chase* (1946) d Arthur Ripley, sc Philip Yordan, n *The Black Path of Fear* Cornell Woolrich, ph Franz Planer, c Michelle Morgan, Robert Cummings. Nightmare Noir of man on run with racketeer's wife.

*Chicago Confidential* (1957) d Sidney Salkow, sc Bernard Gordon, st Hugh King, book Jack Lait, Lee Mortimer, ph Kenneth Peach, c Brian Keith. Mobs take over the union.

*Chicago Deadline* (1949) d Lewis Allen, sc Warren Duff, n *One Woman* Tiffany Thayer, ph John F Seitz, c Alan Ladd. Chicago reporter obsessed with dead girl's past.

*Chinatown at Midnight* (1949) d Seymour Friedman, sc Frank Burt, Robert Libott, ph Henry Freulich, c Hurd Hatfield.

*Christmas Holiday* (1944) d Robert Siodmak, sc Herman J Mankiewicz, n Somerset Maugham, ph John P Fulton, c Deanna Durbin, Gene Kelly. Girl tells soldier of her tragic marriage.

*Circumstantial Evidence* (1945) d John Larkin, sc Robert Metzler, ad Samuel Ornitz, st Nat Ferber, Sam Duncan, ph Harry Jackson, c Michael O'Shea. Innocent reporter escapes from prison on eve of execution.

*City Across the River* (1949) d Maxwell Shane, sc Shane, Dennis Cooper, n *The Amboy Dukes* Irving Shulman, ph Maury Gertsman, c Stephan McNally. Juvenile Delinquent Noir of teacher accidentally murdered.

*City for Conquest* (1941) d Anatole Litvak, sc John Wexley, ph Sol Polito, James Wong Howe, c James Cagney, Ann Sheridan.

*City of Chance* (1940) d Ricardo Cortez, sc John Larkin, Barry Trivers, ph Lucien N Andriot, c Lynn Bari. Texas girl tries to get gambling boyfriend out of New York.

*City of Fear* (1959) d Irving Lerner, sc Steven Ritch, Robert Dillon, ph Lucien Ballard, c Vince Edwards. Escaped convict steals radioactive material thinking it is heroin.

*City of Shadows* (1955) d William Whitney, sc Houston Branch, ph Reggie Lanning, c John Baer.

*City that Never Sleeps* (1953) d John H Auer, sc Steve Fisher, ph John L Russell, c Gig Young. Chicago cop is tempted by corruption.

*Clash by Night* (1952) d Fritz Lang, sc Alfred Hayes, pl Clifford Odets, ph Nicholas Musuraca, c Barbara Stanwyck, Robert Ryan. Melodrama Noir as woman is caught between two men. 3/5

*The Clay Pigeon* (1949) d Richard Fleischer, sc Carl Foreman, ph Robert de Grasse, c Bill Williams. Nightmare Noir. Amnesic man wakes and is accused of being war traitor.

*The Come-On* (1956) d Russell Birdwell, sc Warren Douglas, Whitman Chambers, n Chambers, ph Ernest Haller, c Anne Baxter, Sterling Hayden. Femme fatale Noir.

*Confidential Report* (1955, *Mr Arkadin*) d sc n Orson Welles, ph Jean Bourgon, c Orson Welles. Mercenary adventurer uses daughter of mysterious financier to find out dark secrets. 3/5

*Conflict* (1945) d Curtis Bernhardt, sc Arthur T Horman, Dwight Taylor, st Robert Siodmak, Alfred Neumann, ph Merritt Gerstad, c Humphrey Bogart. Man murders wife then lusts after sister.

*Convicted* (1950) d Henry Levin, sc William Bowers, Fred

Nibbo, Seton I Miller, pl Martin Flavin, ph Burnett Guffey, c Glenn Ford, Broderick Crawford. Innocent man becomes hardened by prison life. Remake of *The Criminal Code* (1932).

*Cop Hater* (1958) d William A Berke, sc Henry Kane, n Ed McBain, ph J Burgi Contner, c Robert Loggia. Detectives of the 87th Precinct hunt a cop killer.

*Cornered* (1945) d Edward Dmytryk, sc John Paxton, st John Wexley, ph Harry J Wild, c Dick Powell. War vet wants revenge for wife's murder. and becomes progressively alienated. 4/5

*Crack-Up* (1946) d Irving Reis, sc John Paxton, Ben Bengal, Ray Spencer, st Fredric Brown, ph Robert de Grasse, c Pat O'Brien, Claire Trevor. Nightmare Noir set in art world. 4/5

*Crashout* (1955) d Lewis Foster, sc Hal E Chester, Foster, ph Russell Metty, c William Bendix. Six men escape from prison.

*Crime Against Joe* (1956) d Lee Sholem, sc Robert C Dennis, st Decla Dunning, ph William Margulies, c John Bromfield, Julie London. Bohemian artist must be proved innocent.

*Crime in the Streets* (1956) d Don Seigel, sc Reginald Rose, ph Sam Leavitt, c John Cassavetes, Sal Mineo. Juvenile delinquent drama.

*Crime of Passion* (1957) d Gerd Oswald, sc Jo Eisinger, ph Joseph La Shelle, c Barbara Stanwyck, Sterling Hayden. Class Noir as cop's wife is unstoppable in quest for husband's promotion.

*Crime Wave* (1954) d André de Toth, sc Crane Wilbur, ad Bernard Gordon, Richard Wormser, st John, Ward Hawkins, ph Bert Glennon, c Gene Nelson, Sterling Hayden. Rehabilitated ex-con dragged back into the life by criminal friends.

*Criminal Court* (1946) d Robert Wise, sc Lawrence Kimble, st

Earl Felton, ph Frank Redman, c Troy Conway. Ambitious
lawyer accidentally kills criminal but girlfriend is accused of
murder.

*The Crimson Kimono* (1959) d sc Sam Fuller, ph Sam Leavitt, c
Victoria Shaw, Glenn Corbett, James Shigeta. Police thriller
about detectives (one Japanese-American) investigating
murder using racial identity as subtext. 3/5

*Criss Cross* (1949) d Robert Siodmak, sc Daniel Fuchs, n Don
Tracy, ph Franz Planer, c Burt Lancaster, Yvonne DeCarlo,
Dan Duryea. Heist Noir. Man obsessed with ex-wife so
does robbery for her new husband. 5/5

*The Crooked Way* (1949) d Robert Florey, sc Richard H
Landau, radio pl Robert Monroe, ph John Alton, c John
Payne. Amnesic war vet discovers past life in LA.

*The Crooked Web* (1955) d Nathan Juran, sc st Lou Breslow, ph
Henry Freulich, c Frank Lovejoy. Man returns to Germany
for treasure.

*Crossfire* (1947) d Edward Dmytryk, sc John Paxton, n *The
Brick Foxhole* Richard Brooks, ph J Roy Hunt, c Robert
Young, Robert Mitchum, Robert Ryan, Gloria Grahame.
Racial Noir featuring war buddies, one of whom kills Jews.
4/5

*Crossroads* (1942) d Jack Conway, sc Guy Trosper, st John
Kafka, Howard Emmett Rogers, ph Joseph Ruttenberg, c
William Powell. French diplomat is amnesic and accused of
murder.

*The Cruel Tower* (1956) d Lew Landers, sc Warren Douglas, n
William B Hartley, ph Ernest Haller, c Steve Brodie.
Problems building a skyscraper.

*Cry Danger* (1951) d Robert Parrish, sc William Bowers, st
Jerome Cady, ph Joseph F Biroc, c Dick Powell. Revenge
Noir for man framed for robbery.

*A Cry in the Night* (1956) d Frank Tuttle, sc Frank Dortort, n
*All Through the Night* Whit Masterson, ph John F Seitz, c

Edmond O'Brien. Police hunt mental killer of girl.

*Cry of the City* (1948) d Robert Siodmak, sc Richard Murphy, n *The Chair for Martin Rome* Henry Edward Helseth, ph Lloyd Ahern, c Victor Mature, Richard Conte. Amoral Noir. Criminal hunted by cop – they were childhood friends.

*Cry of the Hunted* (1953) d Joseph H Lewis, sc Jack Leonard, ph Harry Lipstein, c Vittorio Gassman, Barry Sullivan.

*Cry Terror* (1958) d sc Andrew L Stone, ph Walter Strenge, c James Mason. Psychopath holds family hostage.

*Cry Tough* (1959) d Paul Stanley, sc Harry Kleiner, n *Children of the Dark* Irving Shulman, ph Philip Lathrop, c John Saxon. Delinquent Noir. Teenager lured into the bad life.

*Cry Vengeance* (1954) d Mark Stevens, sc Warren Douglas, George Bricker, ph William Sickner, c Mark Stevens. Innocent ex-con seeks revenge on framers who murdered his family.

*Cry Wolf* (1947) d Peter Godfrey, sc Catherine Turney, n Marjorie Carleton, ph Carl Guthrie, c Errol Flynn, Barbara Stanwyck. Gothic Noir. Woman claims to be heir of country estate.

*The Damned Don't Cry* (1950) d Vincent Sherman, sc Harold Medford, Jerome Weidman, st Gertrude Walker, ph Ted McCord, c Joan Crawford. Class Noir. Woman claws way to top.

*Danger Signal* (1945) d Robert Florey, sc Adele Commandini, Graham Baker, n Phyllis Bottome, ph James Wong Howe, c Faye Emerson, Zachary Scott. Artist provokes two sisters to fight.

*Dangerous Crossing* (1953) d Joseph M Newman, sc Leo Townsend, st John Dickson Carr, ph Joseph La Shelle, c Jeanne Crain, Michael Rennie. Woman's husband disappears on honeymoon.

*A Dangerous Profession* (1949) d Ted Tetzlaff, sc Martin Rackin,

Warren Duff, ph Robert de Grasse, c George Raft. Woman asks bail bondsman to help her husband.

*Dark City* (1950) d William Dieterle, sc John Meredith Lucas, Larry Marcus, ad Marcus, ph Victor Milner, c Charlton Heston, Lizabeth Scott. Moral Noir. Gambler hunted by psycho brother of man he swindled and who subsequently committed suicide.

*The Dark Corner* (1946) d Henry Hathaway, sc Jay Dratler, Bernard Schoenfeld, st Leo Rosten, ph Joe MacDonald, c Mark Stevens, Lucille Ball. PI devastated as he becomes pawn in murder plot. 5/5

*The Dark Mirror* (1946) d Robert Siodmak, sc Nunnally Johnson, st Vladimir Pozner, ph Milton Krasner, c Olivia De Havilland, Lew Ayres. Doppelgänger Noir. Which twin sister committed murder?

*Dark Passage* (1947) d sc Delmar Daves, n David Goodis, ph Sid Hickox, c Humphrey Bogart, Lauren Bacall. Escaped convict/innocent man seeks plastic surgery and revenge. 4/5

*The Dark Past* (1948) d Rudolph Maté, sc Philip MacDonald, Michael Blankfort, Albert Duffy, ad Malvin Wald, Oscar Saul, pl James Warwick, ph Joseph Walker, c William Holden. Remake of *Blind Alley* (1939)

*Dark Waters* (1944) d André de Toth, sc Joan Harrison, Marion Cockrell, st Frank, Marion Cockrell, ph Archie Stout, John Mescall, c Merle Oberon, Franchot Tone. Psychological Noir. Woman begins to hear voices.

*Date with Death* (1959) d Harold Daniels, sc Robert C Dennis, ph Carl E Guthrie, c Gerald Mohr. Hobo takes on identity of dead cop and then assigned to clean up gangster-ridden town.

*Dead Reckoning* (1947) d John Cromwell, sc Oliver H P Garrett, Steve Fisher, ad Allen Rivkin, st Gerald Adams, Sidney Biddell, ph Leo Tover, c Humphrey Bogart, Lizabeth

Scott. War vet investigates buddy's murder and falls for femme fatale.

*Deadline at Dawn* (1946) d Harold Clurman, sc Clifford Odets, n Cornell Woolrich, ph Nicholas Musuraca, c Susan Hayward. Nightmare Noir. Overnight, woman helps sailor fight upcoming murder charge. Stunning photography, great walk-on cast. 4/5

*Death of a Scoundrel* (1956) d sc Charles Martin, ph James Wong Howe, c George Sanders, Yvonne De Carlo. Rich women relieved of wealth by charmer.

*Deception* (1946) d Irving Rapper, sc John Collier, Joseph Than, pl Louis Verneuil, ph Ernest Haller, c Bette Davis, Paul Henreid, Claude Rains. Woman caught between two men.

*Decoy* (1946) d Jack Bernhard, sc Ned Young, st Stanley Rubin, ph L W O'Connell, c Jean Gillie. Femme fatale saves gangster from execution to grab his money.

*Deep Valley* (1947) d Jean Negulesco, sc Salka Viertel, Stephen Morehouse Avery, n Dan Totheroh, ph Ted McCord, c Ida Lupino. Convict sheltered by country girl.

*Desert Fury* (1947) d Lewis Allen, sc A I Bezzerides, Robert Rossen, n *Desert Town* Ramona Stewart, ph Edward Cronjager, Charles Lang, c John Hodiak, Lizabeth Scott, Burt Lancaster, Mary Astor. Casinos, gambling, murder, intrigue.

*Desperate* (1947) d Anthony Mann, sc Harry Essex, st Dorothy Atlas, Mann, ph George E Diskant, c Steve Brodie, Audrey Long. Nightmare Noir. Truck driver tricked by gang, and on run with wife.

*Desperate Hours* (1955) d William Wyler, sc pl n Joseph Hayes, ph Lee Garmes, c Humphrey Bogart, Frederic March. Three convicts hide out in middle-class home.

*Destination Murder* (1950) d Edward L Cahn, sc Don Martin, ph Jackson J Rose, c Joyce MacKenzie. Woman hunts father's killers.

*Destiny* (1944) d Reginald LeBorg (& Julien Duvivier), sc Roy Chanslor, Ernest Pascal, ph George Robinson, c Gloria Jean. Melodrama Noir. Man exploited by people whilst on the run.

*Detective Story* (1951) d William Wyler, sc Philip Yordan, Robert Wilder, pl Sidney Kingsley, ph Lee Garmes, c Kirk Douglas, Eleanor Parker, William Bendix. Melodrama Noir. Home and professional life clash for cop. 4/5

*Detour* (1945) d Edgar G Ulmer, sc Martin Goldsmith, ph Benjamin H Kline, c Tom Neal. Nightmare Noir. Man destined to be at two freak accidents – fate against him. 5/5

*The Devil's Sleep* (1949) d W Merle Connell, sc Danny Arnold, Richard S McMahan, ph William C Thompson, c Lita Grey, John Mitchum, Timothy Farrell. Crusading judge is blackmailed by seedy conman.

*The Devil Thumbs a Ride* (1947) d sc Felix Feist, n Robert C DuSoe, ph J Roy hunt, c Lawrence Tierney. Nightmare Noir. Man gives lift to criminal on the run.

*Dial 1119* (1950) d Gerald Mayer, sc John Monks Jr, st Hugh King, Don McGuire, ph Paul C Vogel, c Marhsall Thompson. Escaped psycho holds bar hostage.

*Dillinger* (1945) d Max Nosseck, sc Philip Yordan, William Castle, ph Jackson Rose, c Lawrence Tierney. Lean retelling of gangster's rise with great Tierney debut.

*Dishonored Lady* (1947) d Robert Stevenson, sc Edmund H North, Ben Hecht, André de Toth, pl Margaret Ayer Barnes, Edward Sheldon, ph Lucien N Andriot, c Hedy Lamarr, Dennis O Keefe. Heading for a breakdown, a society girl adopts a new identity and gets involved with murder.

*The Dividing Line* (1950, *The Lawless* in US) d Joseph Losey, sc n *The Voice of Stephen Wilder* Geoffrey Homes, ph J Roy Hunt, c Macdonald Carey. Small Town/Racial Noir. Mexican hits cop and situation escalates.

*DOA* (1950) d Rudolph Maté, sc Russell Rouse, Clarence

Greene, ph Ernest Lazlo, c Edmond O'Brien. Nightmare Noir. Poisoned man has hours to hunt his own killer. 4/5

*Don't Bother to Knock* (1952) d Roy Baker, sc Daniel Taradash, n *Mischief* Charlotte Armstrong, ph Lucien Ballard, c Richard Widmark, Marilyn Monroe. Disillusioned man meets beautiful (but deadly) girl.

*Don't Gamble with Strangers* (1946) d William Beaudine, sc Caryl Coleman, Harvey Gates, ph William A Sickner, c Kane Richmond

*Double Indemnity* (1944) d Billy Wilder, sc Wilder, Raymond Chandler, n James M Cain, ph John F Seitz, c Fred MacMurray, Edward G Robinson, Barbara Stanwyck. Man and woman murder her husband for money. 5/5

*A Double Life* (1948) d George Cukor, sc Ruth Gordon, Garson Kanin, ph Milton Krasner, c Ronald Coleman. Actor becomes Othello.

*Dragonwyck* (1946) d sc Joseph L Mankiewicz, n Anya Seton, ph Arthur C Miller, c Gene Tierney, Walter Huston, Vincent Price. Gothic Noir.

*Drive a Crooked Road* (1954) d ad Richard Quine, sc Black Edwards, st James Benson, ph Charles Lawton, c Mickey Rooney. Man persuaded by femme fatale to drive getaway car.

*Edge of Doom* (1950) d Mark Robson, sc Philip Yordan, n Leo Brady, ph Harry Stradling, c Dana Andrews, Farley Granger. Social Noir. Poor man strikes back via murder.

*Edge of Fury* (1958) d Robert J Gurney Jr, Irving Lerner, sc Gurney, Ted Berkman, n *Wisteria Cottage* Robert M Coates, ph Jack Couffer, Conrad L Hall, Marvin R Weinstein, c Malcolm Lee Beggs. Story of madness and murder. Beggs was murdered two years before the film was released.

*Edge of the City* (1957) d Martin Ritt, sc Robert Allan Aurthur, ph Joseph C Brun, c John Cassavetes, Sidney Poitier. Set on the New York docks, this is a Social Noir.

*End of the Road* (1944) d George Blair, ph William Bradford, c Edward Norris.

*The Enforcer* (1951, *Murder Inc* in UK) d Bretaigne Windust (& Raoul Walsh), sc Martin Rackin, ph Robert Burks, c Humphrey Bogart. Docu Noir. DA seeks witness to close down professional hit man business.

*Escape* (1948) d Joseph L Mankiewicz, sc Philip Dunne, pl John Galsworthy, ph Frederick A Young, c Rex Harrison. After accidental killing, man escapes prison and meets girl.

*Escape in the Fog* (1945) d Budd Boetticher, sc Aubrey Wiseberg, ph George Meehan, c Nina Foch. Nightmare Noir. Nurse dreams murder then meets victim.

*Experiment Perilous* (1944) d Jacques Tourneur, sc Warren Duff, n Margaret Carpenter, ph Tony Gaudio, c Hedy Lamarr. Gothic Noir. Woman held prisoner by husband.

*A Face in the Crowd* (1957) d Elia Kazan, sc Budd Schulberg, c Andy Griffith, Patricia Neal. Great, great con movie. 5/5

*Fall Guy* (1947) d Reginald LeBorg, sc Jerry Warner, st *Cocaine* Cornell Woolrich, ph Mack Stengler, c Clifford Penn. Amnesic man tries to prove himself innocent of murder.

*Fallen Angel* (1946) d Otto Preminger, sc Harry Kleiner, n Marty Holland, ph Joseph La Shelle, c Dana Andrews, Alice Faye, Linda Darnell. Amoral Noir. Traveller marries money so he can be with lover, but wife is killed. 4/5

*The Fallen Sparrow* (1943) d Richard Wallace, sc Warren Duff, n Dorothy B Hughes, ph Nicholas Musuraca, c John Garfield, Maureen O'Hara. Nightmare Noir. 4/5

*Farewell, My Lovely* (1944, *Murder My Sweet*) d Edward Dmytryk, sc John Paxton, n Raymond Chandler, ph Harry J Wild, c Dick Powell, Claire Trevor. PI Philip Marlowe tells police how he unmasked femme fatale. 5/5

*The Fatal Witness* (1945) d Lesley Selander, sc Cleve F Adams, Jerry Sackheim, pl Banquo's Chair Rupert Croft-Cooke, ph Bud Thackery, c Richard Fraser.

*Fear* (1946) d Alfred Zeisler, sc Zeisler, Dennis Cooper, ph Jackson Rose, c Warren William. Medical student kills professor and irony ensues.

*Fear in the Night* (1947) d sc Maxwell Shane, st *Nightmare* Cornell Woolrich, ph Jack Greenhalgh, c Paul Kelly. After dreaming a murder, man wakes to find murder happened!

*The Fearmakers* (1958) d Jacques Tournear, sc Chris Appley, Elliot West, n Darwin L Teilhet, ph Sam Leavitt, c Dana Andrews. Korean vet returns home to find there is a conspiracy to use his PR agency to manipulate the American public. Paranoid Noir.

*Female Jungle* (1955) d Bruno Ve Sota, sc Burt Kaiser, Ve Sota, ph Elwood Bredell, c Lawrence Tierney, John Carradine.

*Female on the Beach* (1955) d Joseph Pevney, sc Robert Hill, Richard Alan Simmons, pl Hill, ph Charles Lang, c Joan Crawford, Jeff Chandler. Domestic Noir. Woman fears neighbour is murderer.

*The File on Thelma Jordon* (1950) d Robert Siodmak, sc Ketti Frings, st Marty Holland, ph George Barnes, c Barbara Stanwyck. DA tries to help his lover beat murder charge. 4/5

*Fingerman* (1955) d Harold D Shuster, sc Warren Douglas, s Norris Lipsius, John Lardner, ph William A Sickner, c Frank Lovejoy, Forrest Tucker, Tomothy Carey. Con goes undercover to catch druglord.

*Fingers at the Window* (1942) d Charles Lederer, sc Lawrence P Bachmann, Rose Caylor, ph Charles Lawton, Harry Stradling Sr, c Lew Ayres, Laraine Day, Basil Rathbone. Lunatic axe-murderers are killing people.

*Five Against the House* (1955) d Phil Karlson, c Guy Madison. Kim Novak, Brian Keith. Heist Noir.

*The Flame* (1947) d John H Auer, sc Lawrence Kimble, st Robert T Shannon, ph Reggie Lanning, c John Carroll. Man persuades nurse to marry his brother for money.

*Flamingo Road* (1949) d Michael Curtiz, sc Robert Wilder, pl Robert, Sally Wilder, ph Ted McCord, c Joan Crawford, Zachary Scott. Melodrama Noir. Dancer marries money then gets caught in web of deceit.

*Flaxy Martin* (1949) d Richard Bare, sc David Lang, ph Carl Guthrie, c Virginia Mayo, Zachary Scott. Attorney confesses to murder femme fatale committed.

*Follow Me Quietly* (1949) d Richard Fleicher, sc Lillie Hayward, st Francis Rosenwald, Anthony Mann, ph Robert de Grasse, c William Lundigan. Cop hunts psychokiller.

*Footsteps in the Night* (1957) d Jean Yarborough, sc Albert Band, Elwood Ullman, st Band, ph Harry Neumann, c Bill Elliott. Police detective believes wrong man charged.

*For You I Die* (1948) d John Reinhardt, sc Robert Presnell Sr, ph William Clothier, c Cathy Downs. Convict on run shelters in diner.

*Forbidden* (1954) d Rudolph Maté, sc William Sackheim, Gil Doud, ph William Daniels, c Tony Curtis. Man hired by mobster to find girlfriend.

*Force of Evil* (1948) d Abraham Polonsky, sc Polonsky, Ira Wolfert, n *Tucker's People* Wolfert, ph George Barnes, c John Garfield. Anti-Capitalist Noir. Crooked lawyer realises how bad he is with death of brother. 5/5

*Four Boys and a Gun* (1957) d William A Berke, sc Philip Yordan, Leo Townsend, n Willard Wiener, ph J Burgi Contner. Four boys killed a cop but only one pulled the trigger. They have to decide which one gets the electric chair.

*Fourteen Hours* (1951) d Henry Hathaway, sc John Paxton, st Joel Sayre, ph Joe MacDonald, c Richard Basehart, Barbara Bel Geddes. Man on ledge of building, threatens to jump. Superb photography and tense direction. 4/5

*Framed* (1947) d Richard Wallace, sc Ben Maddow, st Jack Patrick, ph Burnett Guffey, c Glenn Ford. Man falls for femme fatale who frames him for embezzlement.

*The Fugitive* (1947) d John Ford, sc Dudley Nichols, n *The Power and the Glory* Graham Greene, ph Gabirel Figueroa, c Henry Fonda, Dolores Del Rio. Man on the Run. 4/5

*Gambling House* (1951) d Ted Tetzlaff, sc Marvin Borowsky, Allen Rivkin, ph Harry Wild, c Victor Mature. Corrupt gambler turns on killer boss.

*The Gangster* (1947) d Gordon Wiles, sc n *Low Company* Daniel Fuchs, ph Paul Icano, c Barry Sullivan. Intense Noir. Gangster loses grip on reality. 4/5

*The Garment Jungle* (1957) d Vincent Sherman (& Robert Aldrich), sc Harry Kleiner, ar Lester Velie, ph Joseph Biroc, c Lee J Cobb. Socialist Noir. Son learns of father's oppressive working practices in dress manufacturer.

*Gaslight* (1944) d George Cukor, sc Walter Reisch, John L Balderston, pl Patrick Hamilton, c Ingrid Bergman, Charles Boyer, Joseph Cotten. Victorian Noir. Man tries to drive wife mad.

*The Get-Away* (1941) d Edward Buzzell, Robert Rossen, sc W R Burnett, Wells Root, s Wells Root, J Walter Ruben, ph Sidney Wagner, c Robert Sterling, Donna Reed. Gangster Noir.

*Gilda* (1946) d Charles Vidor, sc Marion Parsonnet, ad Jo Eisinger, st E A Ellington, ph Rudolph Maté, c Rita Hayworth, Glenn Ford. Gambler earns trust of casino owner, then falls for owner's femme fatale wife. 4/5

*Girl in 313* (1940) d Ricardo Cortez, sc M Clay Adams, Barry Trivers, st Hilda Stone, ph Edward Cronjager, c Florence Rice. Girl goes undercover with jewel thieves but falls for one of the gang.

*The Girl in Black Stockings* (1957) d Howard W Koch, sc Richard H Landau, st *Wanton Murder* Peter Godfrey, ph William Margulies, c Mamie Van Doren, Marie Windsor, Anne Bancroft. Blonde is killed and everybody is suspect.

*The Girl on the Bridge* (1951) d Hugo Haas, sc Haas, Arnold Phillips, ph Paul Ivano, c Haas, Beverly Michaels. Man saves woman from suicide, but she has a dark past.

*The Glass Alibi* (1946) d W Lee Wilder, sc Mindret Lord, ph Henry Sharp, c Paul Kelly. Reporter marries dying woman for money, but she lives so he plans her murder.

*The Glass Key* (1942) d Stuart Heisler, sc Jonathan Latimer, n Dashiell Hammett, ph Theodor Sparkuhl, c Brian Donlevy, Veronica Lake, Alan Ladd. Political Noir. Politican's aide fights racketeer and clears boss of murder.

*The Glass Wall* (1953) d Maxwell Shane, sc Ivan Tors, Shane, ph Joseph F Biroc, c Vittorio Gassmann, Gloria Grahame. Man goes on run when officials refuse him entry into US.

*The Glass Web* (1953) d Jack Arnold, sc Robert Blees, Leonard Lee, n Max S Ehrlich, ph Maury Gertsman, c Edward G Robinson. Expert for TV crime show knows too much about one particular murder.

*The Great Flamarion* (1945) d Anthony Mann, sc Heinz Herald, Richard Weil, Anne Wigton, st *The Big Shot* Vicki Baum, ph James S Brown Jr, c Erich Von Stroheim, Mary Beth Hughes, Dan Duryea. *Double Indemnity* at a variety show.

*Grand Central Murder* (1942) d S Sylvan Simon, sc Peter Ruric, n Susan MacVeigh, ph George J Folsey, c Van Heflin. PI solves a whodunit at the New York train station.

*The Green Buddha* (1955) d John Lemont, sc Paul Erickson, ph Basil Emmott, c Wayne Morris.

*The Green Glove* (1952) d Rudolph Maté, sc st Charles Bennett, ph Claude Renoir, c Glenn Ford. Ex-GI returns to France for priceless antique, religious object.

*Guest in the House* (1944) d John Brahm (& Lewis Milestone, André de Toth), sc Ketti Frings, pl Hager Wilder, Dale Eunson, ph Lee Garmes, c Anne Baxter. Psychological Noir. Disturbed girl affects household.

*The Guilty* (1947) d John Reinhardt, sc Robert S Presnell Sr, st *Two Men in a Furnished Room* Cornell Woolrich, ph Henry Sharp, c Bonita Granville. Doppelgänger Noir. Twin sisters love same man.

*Guilty Bystander* (1950) d Joseph Lerner, sc Don Ettlinger, n Wade Miller, ph Gerald Hirschfeld, c Zachary Scott. Ex-cop/drunkard searches seedy lowlife dives for ex-wife's kidnapped son.

*Gun Crazy* (1950, *Deadly is the Female*) d Joseph H Lewis, sc MacKinlay Kantor, Millard Kaufman, st Kantor, ph Russell Harlan, c Peggy Cummins, John Dahl. Obsessive Noir. Two gun freak lovers go on robbery rampage to the death. 5/5

*Hangover Square* (1945) d John Brahm, sc Barre Lyndon, n Patrick Hamilton, ph Joseph La Shelle, c Laird Cregar, Linda Darnell. Schizo Noir. Composer leads double life, obsessed by whore, kills in anger. 4/5

*The Harder they Fall* (1956) d Mark Robson, sc Philip Yordan, n Budd Schulberg, ph Burnett Guffey, c Humphrey Bogart, Rod Steiger. Sportwriter becomes disgusted by corrupt boxing scene.

*He Ran All the Way* (1951) d John Berry, sc Guy Endore, Hugo Butler, n Sam Ross, ph James Wong Howe, c John Garfield. Criminal on run hides out with family. 4/5

*He Walked By Night* (1948) d Alfred Werker (& Anthony Mann), sc John C Higgins, Crane Wilbur, st Wilbur, ph John Alton, c Richard Basehart. Docu Noir. Cops hunt psycho who kills at night. 4/5

*Hell's Half Acre* (1954) d John H Auer, sc Steve Fisher, ph John L Russell, c Wendell Corey, Evelyn Keyes, Elsa Lanchester, Marie Windsor. Women hunts for lost husband in Hawaii but finds murder.

*Hell's Island* (1955) d Phil Karlson, sc Maxwell Shane, st Jack Leonard, Martin M Goldsmith, ph Lionel Lindon, c John Payne. Alcoholic ex-attorney hired by wheelchair-bound financier to recover ruby.

*Her Kind of Man* (1946) d Frederick de Cordova, sc Gordon
Kahn, Leopold Atlas, st Charles Hoffman, James V Kern, ph
Carl Guthrie, c Dane Clark. Singer is caught between two
men (gangster, columnist).

*High Sierra* (1941) d Raoul Walsh, sc John Huston, W R
Burnett, n Burnett, ph Tony Gaudio, c Humphrey Bogart,
Ida Lupino. Last job goes wrong for old criminal as he is
pursued by fate. 5/5

*High Tide* (1947) d John Reinhardt, sc Robert Presnell Sr, ph
Henry Sharp, c Lee Tracy. Reporter caught in power
struggle for city.

*High Wall* (1947) d Curtis Bernhardt, sc Sydney Boehm, Lester
Cole, n pl Alan R Clark, Bradbury Foote, ph Paul C Vogel,
c Robert Taylor, Audrey Totter. War vet blacks out and is
arrested for wife's murder then goes to asylum to buy time.

*Highway Dragnet* (1954) d Nathan Juran, sc U S Anderson,
Roger Corman, ph John Martin, c Richard Conte, Joan
Bennett. Femme fatale gives lift to innocent war vet on run.

*Highway 301* (1950) d sc Andrew L Stone, ph Carl Guthrie, c
Steve Cochran. Docu Noir. Robbery gang on warpath.

*His Kind of Woman* (1951) d John Farrow, sc Frank Fenton,
Jack Leonard, st Gerald Drayson Adams, ph Harry J Wild, c
Robert Mitchum, Jane Russell. Gambler tangles with bad
people in Mexico.

*Hit and Run* (1957) d sc Hugo Hass, ph Walter Strenge, c Cleo
Moore, Hugo Haas, Vince Edwards.

*The Hitch-Hiker* (1953) d Ida Lupino, sc Collier Young,
Lupino, ad Robert Joseph, st Daniel Mainwaring, ph
Nicholas Musuraca, c Edmond O'Brien. Psycho holds two
men hostage.

*Hold Back Tomorrow* (1955) d sc Hugo Haas, ph Paul Ivano, c
John Agar, Cleo Moore. Man about to hang for strangling
women is given a last request – to have a woman in his cell
for a night!

*Hollow Triumph* (1948, *The Scar*) d Steve Sekely, sc Daniel Fuchs, n Murray Forbes, ph John Alton, c Paul Henreid, Joan Bennett. Doppelgänger Noir. Alienated criminal tries to become his psychiatrist.

*Hollywood Story* (1951) d William Castle, sc Frederick Kohner, Fred Brady, ph Carl Guthrie, c Richard Conte. 1929 murder of Hollywood director made the subject of a film.

*Homicide* (1949) d Felix Jacoves, sc William Sackheim, ph J Peverell Marley, c Robert Douglas. Cop takes leave of absence to investigate murder.

*The Hoodlum* (1951) d Max Nosseck, sc Sam Neuman, Nat Tanchuck, ph Clark Ramsey, c Lawrence Tierney. Ex-con plans for brother to take blame for bank robbery.

*Hoodlum Empire* (1952) d Joseph Kane, sc Bruce Manning, Bob Considine, st Considine, ph Reggie Lanning, c Brian Donlevy, Claire Trevor. War vet no longer with pre-war gang but they use his name anyway.

*The House Across the Bay* (1940) d Archie Mayo, Alfred Hitchcock, sc Myles Connolly, Kathryn Scola, ph Merritt B Gerstad, c George Raft, Joan Bennett. Man falls for wife of criminal, and then the criminal gets out of jail.

*House by the River* (1950) d Fritz Lang, sc Mel Dinelli, n A P Herbert, ph Edward Cronjagger, c Louis Harward, Jane Wyatt. After accidental killing, writer takes progressively violent action to cover up. 4/5

*House of Bamboo* (1955) d Sam Fuller, sc Harry Kleiner, additional dialogue Sam Fuller, ph Joe MacDonald, c Robert Ryan, Robert Stack. Remake of *Street With No Name*. Man infiltrates robbery gang of former soldiers. 4/5

*House of Numbers* (1957) d Russell Rouse, sc Rouse, Don Mankiewicz, n Jack Finney, ph George J Folsey, c Jack Palance.

*House of Strangers* (1949) d Joseph L Mankiewicz, sc Philip Yordan, n *I'll Never Go There Again* Jerome Weidman, ph

Milton Krasner, c Edward G Robinson, Susan Hayward, Richard Conte. Melodrama Noir. Banker father turns four sons on each other. (Opening prowling camera 'stolen' by Coen Brothers for *Miller's Crossing*.) 4/5

*The House on 92nd Street* (1945) d Henry Hathaway, sc Barre Lyndon, Charles G Booth, John Monks Jr, st Booth, ph Norbert Brodine, c William Eythe, Lloyd Nolan. The first Docu Noir. FBI breaks up Nazi spy ring.

*House on Telegraph Hill* (1951) d Robert Wise, sc Elick Moll, Frank Partos, n *The Frightened Child* Dana Lyon, ph Lucien Ballard, c Richard Basehart. WW2 refugee takes identity of dead woman to live with rich family.

*The Houston Story* (1952) d William Castle, sc Robert E Kent (James B Gordon), ph Henry Freulich, c Gene Barry. Wildcatter dreams up scheme to siphon off oil and sell it.

*Human Desire* (1954) d Fritz Lang, sc Alfred Hayes, n *La Bête Humaine* Emile Zola, ph Burnett Guffey, c Glenn Ford, Gloria Grahame, Broderick Crawford. Femme fatale persuades man to kill her drunkard husband.

*The Human Jungle* (1954) d Joseph M Newman, sc William Sackheim, Daniel Fuchs, ph Ellis Carter, c Gary Merrill. Cop cleans up dirty city.

*Humoresque* (1947) d Jean Negulesco, sc Clifford Odets, Zachary Gold, st Fannie Hunt, ph Ernest Haller, c Joan Crawford, John Garfield. Melodrama Noir. Young violinist and patroness go head to head.

*Hunt the Man Down* (1950) d George Archainbaud, sc De Vallon Scott, ph Nicholas Musuraca, c Gig Young. Lawyer tracks down seven people involved in 12-year-old crime.

*The Hunted* (1948) d Jack Bernhard, sc Steve Fisher, ph Harry Neumann, c Preston Foster. Obsessive Noir. Cop sends girl-friend to prison then harasses her when she gets out.

*I Confess* (1953) d Alfred Hitchcock, sc George Tabori, William Archibald, pl Paul Anthelme, c Montgomery Clift, Anne

Baxter, Karl Malden. Priest hears confession of murderer then is accused of said murder. 3/5

*I Died a Thousand Times* (1955) d Stuart Heisler, n *High Sierra* W R Burnett, c Jack Palance. Remake of *High Sierra*.

*I, Jane Doe* (1948) d John H Auer, sc Lawrence Kimble, ad Decla Dunning, ph Reggie Lanning, c Ruth Hussey. Anonymous French war bride kills womanising husband.

*I'll Cry Tomorrow* (1955) d Daniel Mann, c Susan Hayward. Biopic of alcoholic actress Lillian Roth.

*Inferno* (1953) d Roy Ward Baker, sc Francis M Cockrell, ph Lucien Ballard, c Robert Ryan. Ruthless businessman is left for dead in the desert by scheming wife and her lover.

*Inner Sanctum* (1948) d Lew Landers, sc James Todd Gollard, ph Allen G Siegler, c Charles Russell, Mary Beth Hughes. A man, a woman and a boy, each with a secret, all end up at a boarding house. Rarely seen, reportedly one to look out for.

*Intrigue* (1947) d Edwin L Marin, sc George F Slavin, Barry Trivers, ph Lucien N Andriot, c George Raft, June Havoc. Asian black market tomfoolery.

*I, the Jury* (1953) d sc Harry Essex, n Mickey Spillane, ph John Alton, c Biff Elliott, Preston Foster. PI Mike Hammer hunts best friend's murderer.

*I Wake Up Screaming* (1941) d H Bruce Humberstone, sc Dwight Taylor n Steve Fisher, ph Edward Cronjagger, c Betty Grable, Victor Mature, Laird Cregar. Man escapes from jail to prove innocence, and is pursued by corrupt cop. 4/5

*I Walk Alone* (1948) d Byron Haskin, sc Charles Schnee, ad Robert Smith, John Bright, pl Theodore Reeves, ph Leo Tover, c Burt Lancaster, Lizabeth Scott, Kirk Douglas. Ex-con wants share of partner's nightclub but ex-friend has other ideas.

*I Want to Live* (1958) d Robert Wise, sc Nelson Gidding, ar Ed Montgomery, letters Barbara Graham, ph Lionel Lindon, c

Susan Hayward. Docu Noir. Possibly innocent woman sent to gas chamber for murder.

*I Was a Communist for the FBI* (1951) d Gordon Douglas, sc Crane Wilbur, st Matt Cvetic, Pete Martin, ph Edwin DuPar, c Frank Lovejoy. Anti-socialist Noir. Steel worker infiltrates Commies.

*I Was a Shoplifter* (1950) d Charles Lamont, sc Irwin Gielgud, ph Irving Glassberg, c Scott Brady.

*I Wouldn't Be In Your Shoes* (1948) d William Nigh, sc Steve Fisher, n Cornell Woolrich, ph Mack Stengler, c Don Castle. Cop helps clear woman's husband of murder. But...

*Illegal* (1955) d Lewis Allen, sc W R Burnett, James R Webb, pl Frank J Collins, ph Peverell Marley, c Edward G Robinson. Remake of *The Mouthpiece* (1933).

*Illegal Entry* (1949) d Frederick de Cordova, sc Joel Malone, ad Art Cohn, st Ben Bengal, Herbert Kline, Dan Moore, ph William Daniels, c Howard Duff. Agents infiltrate smugglers on Mexican border.

*Impact* (1949) d Arthur Lubin, sc Dorothy Reid, Jay Dratler, ph Ernest Laszlo, c Brian Donlevy. Businessman starts anonymous life after wife and her lover try to kill him.

*In a Lonely Place* (1950) d Nicholas Ray, sc Andrew Solt, ad Edmund H North, n Dorothy B Hughes, ph Burnett Guffey, c Humphrey Bogart, Gloria Grahame. Lonely, explosive screenwriter accused of murder and finds love, but fate has finger pointed his way. 5/5

*Incident* (1948) d William Beaudine, sc Fred Niblo Jr, Sam Roca, st Harry Lewis, ph Marcel Le Picard, c Warren Douglas. Nightmare Noir. Man beaten because he looks like gangster. It is just the beginning.

*Inside Job* (1946) d Jean Yarbrough, sc George Bricker, Jerry Warner, st Tod Browning, Garrett Fort, ph Maury Gertsman, c Preston Foster. Ex-con must either lose job or do robbery.

*Iron Man* (1951) d Joseph Pevney, sc George Zuckerman, Borden Chase, st W R Burnett, ph Carl Guthrie, c Jeff Chandler. Tough man thinks boxing is road to riches.

*Ivy* (1947) d Sam Wood, sc Charles Bennett, n *The Story of Ivy* Marie Belloc-Lowndes, ph Russell Metty, c Joan Fontaine. Femme fatale poisons husband and lets lover take blame.

*Jealousy* (1945) d Gustav Machaty, sc Arnold Phillips, Machaty, st Dalton Trumbo, ph Henry Sharp, c John Loder. Alcoholic writer is killed and his loyal wife is accused.

*Jennifer* (1953) d Joel Newton, sc Harold Buchman, Maurice Rapf, st Jane Eberle, ph James Wong Howe, c Ida Lupino, Howard Duff. Poor woman takes job as caretaker of a mysterious mansion.

*Jeopardy* (1953) d John Sturges, sc Mel Dinelli, Maurice Zimm, ph Victor Milner, c Barbara Stanwyck, Barry Sullivan, Ralph Meeker. Nightmare Noir. Looking for help for injured husband; wife is held hostage by killer on run.

*Jigsaw* (1949) d Fletcher Markle, sc Markle, Vincent McConnor, st John Roeburt, ph Don Malkames, c Franchot Tone. Assistant DA investigates girl's murder with photos as only clue.

*Johnny Angel* (1945) d Edwin L Marin, sc Steve Fisher, ad Frank Gruber, n *Mr Angel Comes Aboard* Charles Gordon Booth, ph Harry J Wild, c George Raft, Claire Trevor. Sea captain searches New York for father's killer.

*Johnny Eager* (1942) d Mervyn LeRoy, sc John Lee Mahin, James Edward Grant, st Grant, ph Harold Rosson, c Robert Taylor, Lana Turner. Bad man Eager causes psychological damage to woman in his quest for power.

*Johnny O'Clock* (1947) d sc Robert Rossen, st Milton Homes, ph Burnett Guffey, c Dick Powell, Evelyn Keyes. Casino owner stuck between woman, hoodlum and police. 3/5

*Johnny Stool Pigeon* (1949) d William Castle, sc Robert L Richards, st Henry Jordan, ph Maury Gertsman, c Howard

Duff, Dan Duryea. Agent and convict infiltrate drug smugglers.

*Journey Into Fear* (1943) d Norman Foster (& Orson Welles), sc Joseph Cotten, Orson Welles, n Eric Ambler, ph Karl Struss, c Joseph Cotten, Dolores Del Rio, Orson Welles. Naval engineer flees Europe stalked by Nazi killers aboard steamship. 3/5

*Julie* (1956) d sc Andrew L Stone, ph Fred Jackman Jr, c Doris Day, Louis Jordan, Barry Sullivan. Woman's husband is psycho and could kill her. 2/5

*Kansas City Confidential* (1952) d Phil Karlson, sc George Bruce, Harry Essex, st Harold S Greene, Roland Brown, ph George E Diskant, c John Payne, Coleen Gray, Preston Foster. Ex-con revenges himself against gang who made him take the fall for armoured car robbery.

*Key Largo* (1948) d John Huston, sc Richard Brooks, Huston, pl Maxwell Anderson, ph Karl Freund, c Humphrey Bogart, Edward G Robinson, Lauren Bacall, Lionel Barrymore, Claire Trevor. Gangster holds people hostage while storm stops him escaping. 4/5

*Key Witness* (1947) d Ross Lederman, sc Edward Bock, ad Bock, Raymond L Schrock, st J Donald Wilson, ph Philip Tannura, c John Beal. To avoid murder investigation, man runs, into worse situation.

*The Killer Is Loose* (1956) d Budd Boetticher, sc Harold Medford, st John, Ward Hopkins, ph Lucien Ballard, c Joseph Cotten. Blaming police detective on wife's death, mental convict escapes prison to gain revenge.

*The Killer That Stalked New York* (1950) d Earl McEvoy, sc Harry Essex, st Milton Lehman, ph Joseph Biroc, c Evelyn Keyes. While smuggling diamonds, woman contracts and spreads smallpox.

*The Killers* (1956) d Robert Siodmak, st Anthony Veiller, st Ernest Hemingway, ph Woody Bredell, David S Horsley, c

Burt Lancaster, Edmond O'Brien, Ava Gardner. Man pursued by killers. 4/5

*Killer's Kiss* (1955) d sc ph Stanley Kubrick, c Frank Silvera, Jamie Smith. Boxer and taxi dancer prevented from leaving town by jealous club owner. 2/5

*The Killing* (1956) d Stanley Kubrick, sc Kubrick, Jim Thompson, n *Clean Break* Lionel White, ph Lucien Ballard, c Sterling Hayden, Marie Windsor, Vince Edwards. Meticulously planned racetrack heist is jinxed by personality of robbers. 5/5

*Kill or Be Killed* (1950) d Max Nosseck, sc Lawrence L Goldman, Nosseck, Arnold Phillips, ph J Roy Hunt, c Lawrence Tierney. Innocent man accused of murder hides in South American jungle.

*A Kiss Before Dying* (1956) d Gerd Oswald, sc Lawrence Roman, n Ira Levin, ph Lucien Ballard, c Robert Wagner, Jeffrey Hunter. Materialist Noir. Amoral young man kills to acquire money and status. 4/5

*Kiss Me Deadly* (1955) d Robert Aldrich, sc A I Bezzerides, n Mickey Spillane, ph Ernest Laszlo, c Ralph Meeker. PI Mike Hammer searches for mysterious box. Flawless, violent, gnomic fable. 5/5

*Kiss of Death* (1947) d Henry Hathaway, sc Ben Hecht, Charles Lederer, n Eleazar Lipsky, ph Norbert Brodine, c Victor Mature, Brian Donlevy, Richard Widmark. Man cannot escape criminal past. 3/5

*Kiss the Blood Off My Hands* (1948, *The Unafraid*) d Norman Foster, sc Leonardo Bercovici, ad Bed Maddow, Walter Bernstein, n Gerald Butler, ph Russell Metty, c Joan Fontaine, Burt Lancaster. War vet accidentally kills man in fight and falls for nurse while on the run.

*Kiss Tomorrow Goodbye* (1950) d Gordon Douglas, sc Harry Brown, n Horace McCoy, ph J Peverell Marley, c James Cagney. Intelligent, violent criminal escapes from prison and rips the heart out of America. 4/5

*Knock on Any Door* (1949) d Nicholas Ray, sc Daniel Taradash, John Monks Jr, n Willard Motley, ph Burnett Guffey, c Humphrey Bogart, John Derek. Slum youth put on trial for murder.

*Ladies in Retirement* (1941) d Charles Vidor, sc Garrett Fort, Reginald Denham, pl Denham, Edward Percy, ph George Barnes, c Ida Lupino, Louis Hayward. Woman murders boss to protect a pair of old sisters.

*The Lady from Shanghai* (1948) d sc Orson Welles, n *If I Die Before I Wake* Sherwood King, ph Charles Laton Jr, c Rita Hayworth, Orson Welles. Irish sailor trapped by femme fatale in bizarre tale. 3/5

*Lady in the Lake* (1947) d Robert Montgomery, sc Steve Fisher, n Raymond Chandler, ph Paul C Vogel, c Robert Montgomery, Audrey Totter. PI Philip Marlowe is hired to find missing publisher of crime magazine. The camera IS Philip Marlowe. 4/5

*Lady on a Train* (1945) d Charles David, sc Edmund Beloin, Robert O'Brien, st Leslie Charteris, ph Woody Bredell, c Deanna Durbin, Ralph Bellamy. Musical Comedy Noir. Woman witnesses murder from train and tracks down killer (singing along the way).

*A Lady Without Passport* (1950) d Joseph H Lewis, sc Howard Dimsdale, ad Cyril Hume, st Lawrence Taylor, ph Paul C Vogel, c Hedy Lamarr, John Hodiak. In Cuba, immigration cop persuades femme fatale to help stop smuggling.

*Larceny* (1948) d George Sherman, sc Herbert F Margolis, Louis Morheim, William Bowers, n *The Velvet Fleece* Louis Elby, John Fleming, ph Irving Glassberg, c John Payne, Dan Duryea. Conman persuades war widow to hand over money for war memorial.

*The Last Crooked Mile* (1946) d Philip Ford, sc Jerry Sackheim, ad Jerry Gruskin, pl obert L Richards, ph Alfred S Keller, c

Donald Barry, Ann Savage. PI investigates whereabouts of missing heist money.

*The Last Mile* (1959) d Howard W Koch, sc Milton Subotsky, Seton I Miller, pl John Wexley, ph Joseph Brun, c Mickey Rooney. Prisoners on death row engineer escape. Remake of 1932 film.

*The Las Vegas Story* (1952) d Robert Stevenson, sc Earl Felton, Harry Essex, st Jay Dratler, ph Harry J Wild, c Jane Russell, Victor Mature.

*Laura* (1944) d Otto Preminger, sc Jay Dratler, Samuel Hoffenstein, Betty Reinhardt, n Vera Caspary, ph Joseph La Shelle, c Gene Tierney, Dana Andrews, Clifton Webb. Obsessive Noir. Detective falls for murdered girl. 5/5

*The Lawless* (1950) d Joseph Losey, sc n *The Voice of Stephen Wilder* Daniel Mainwaring (Geoffrey Homes), ph J Roy Hunt, c Macdonald Carey, Gail Russell. Californian news-paperman gets involved in plight of Mexican fruitpickers and raises race issues. Social Noir.

*Leave Her to Heaven* (1945) d John M Stahl, sc Jo Swerling, n Ben Ames Williams, ph Leon Shamroy, c Gene Tierney, Cornel Wilde. Femme fatale will stop at nothing to keep husband, including killing her unborn child and his young brother. 5/5

*The Leopard Man* (1943) d Jacques Tourneur, sc Ardel Wray, Edward Dein, n *Black Alibi* Cornell Woolrich, ph Robert De Grasse, c Dennis O'Keefe. Moody thriller about an escaped leopard that kills.

*The Letter* (1940) d William Wyler, sc Howard Koch, st W Somerset Maugham, ph Tony Gaudio, c Bette Davis. Melodrama Noir. Wife kills lover and lies to avoid prison.

*A Life at Stake* (1954) d Paul Guilfoyle, sc Russ Bender, st Hank McCune, ph Ted Allan, c Angela Lansbury. A husband has strange accidents after his wife has an affair.

*Lifeboat* (1944) d Alfred Hitchcock, sc Jo Swerling, Ben Hecht, st John Steinbeck, ph Glen MacWilliams, c Tallulah Bankhead. People stranded on lifeboat during war must become animals to kill Nazis among them. Social Noir.

*Lightning Strikes Twice* (1951) d King Vidor, sc Lenore Coffee, n *A Man Without Friends* Margaret Echard, ph Sid Hickox, c Richard Todd. After being acquitted of wife's murder, man returns to suspicious home.

*The Lineup* (1958) d Don Seigel, sc Sterling Silliphant, ph Hal Mohr, c Eli Wallach. Professional killers hunt down heroin smuggled into country. 4/5

*Loan Shark* (1952) d Seymour Friedman, sc Martin Rackin, Eugene Ling, st Rackin, ph Joseph Biroc, c George Raft. Ex-con joins loan sharks to avenge brother's death.

*The Locket* (1947) d John Brahm, sc Sheridan Gibney, ph Nicholas Musuraca, c Laraine Day, Brian Aherne, Robert Mitchum. Materialist Noir. Woman wants everything and destroys those around her.

*The Lodger* (1944) d John Brahm, sc Barre Lyndon, n Marie Belloc-Lowndes, ph Lucien Ballard, c Laird Cregar, Merle Oberon, George Sanders. Killer roams Victorian streets killing young women.

*The Long Night* (1947) d Anatole Litvak, sc John Wexley, st Jacques Viot, ph Sol Polito, c Henry Fonda, Barbara Bel Geddes. Killer locks himself in room. Remake of French masterpiece *Le Jour se Lève* (1939).

*The Long Wait* (1954) d Victor Saville, sc Alan Green, Lesser Samuels, n Mickey Spillane, ph Franz Planer, c Anthony Quinn, Charles Coburn. Amnesiac tries to clear himself of murder.

*Loophole* (1954) d Harold D Shuster, sc Warren Douglas, st George Bricker, Dwight Babcock, ph William Sickner, c Barry Sullivan, Charles McGraw. Bank teller hounded by investigator who thinks he is embezzler.

*The Lost Hours* (1952, *The Big Frame*) d David MacDonald, sc

Steve Fisher, John Gilling, s Robert S Baker, Carl Nystrom, ph Monty Berman, c Mark Stevens, Jean Kent. American goes to London for veteran reunion and wakes up accused of murder.

*The Lost Moment* (1947) d Martin Gabel, sc Leonardo Bercovici, n *The Aspern Papers* Henry James, ph Hal Mohr, c Robert Cummings, Susan Hayward. Man hunts love letters to make his literary name but has to deal with gothic house and psychological games to get them.

*The Lost Weekend* (1945) d Billy Wilder, n Charles Jackson, c Ray Milland. Story of alcoholic. 5/5

*Love from a Stranger* (1947) d Richard Whorf, sc Philip MacDonald, pl Frank Vosper, st Agatha Christie, ph Tony Gaudio, c Sylvia Sidney. Wife fears husband will murder her.

*Lured* (1947, *Personal Column*) d Douglas Sirk, sc Leo Rosten, st Jacques Campaneez, Ernest Neuville, Simon Gantillon, ph William Daniels, c George Sanders, Lucille Ball. Girl hunts friend, ends up as bait for killer. Remake of Robert Siodmak's *Pièges* (1939).

*M* (1951) d Joseph Losey, sc Norman Raine, Leo Katcher, based on 1931 sc by Thea Von Harbou, ph Ernest Laszlo, c David Wayne, Howard da Silva. Child-killer hunted by underworld and police alike.

*Macao* (1952) d Josef von Sternberg (& Nicholas Ray), sc Bernard C Shoenfeld, Stanley Rubin, st Bob Williams, ph Harry J Wild, c Robert Mitchum, Jane Russell. War vet on run from US mistaken for detective hunting racketeer.

*The Macomber Affair* (1947) d Zoltan Korda, sc Casey Robinson, ad Seymour Bennett, Frank Arnold, st Ernest Hemingway, ph Karl Struss, c Gregory Peck, Joan Bennett. Safari guide caught between femme fatale and her weak husband.

*Mad at the World* (1955) d sc Harry Essex, ph William E Snyder, c Frank Lovejoy.

*Make Haste to Live* (1954) d William Seiter, sc Warren Duff, n The Gordons, ph John L Russell Jr, c Dorothy McGuire, Stephen McNally.

*The Maltese Falcon* (1941) d sc John Huston, n Dashiell Hammett, ph Arthur Edeson, c Humphrey Bogart, Mary Astor, Peter Lorre, Sydney Greenstreet. PI Sam Spade avenges death of partner and hunts treasure. 4/5

*The Man I Love* (1946) d Raoul Walsh, sc Catherine Turney, Jo Pagano, n *Night Shift* Maritta Wolff, ph Sid Hickox, c Ida Lupino. Melodrama Noir. Maladjusted post-war people centred around nightclub.

*Man in the Attic* (1953) d Hugo Fregonese, sc Barre Lyndon, Robert Presnell Jr, n *The Lodger* Marie Belloc-Lowndes, ph Leo Tover, c Jack Palance. Killer roams Victorian streets killing young women. Again.

*Man in the Dark* (1953) d Lew Landers, sc George Bricker, Jack Leonard, ad William Sackheim, st Tom Van Dycke, Henry Altimus, ph Floyd Crosby, c Edmond O'Brien, Audrey Totter. Concept Noir. Brain operation to remove criminal impulses of convict cause him to lose memory. Then he meets his old gang.

*Man in the Net* (1959) d Michael Curtiz, sc Reginald Rose, st Patrick Quentin, ph John F Seitz, c Alan Ladd. Artist attempts to clear himself of wife's murder.

*The Man is Armed* (1956) d Franklin Adreon, sc Richard Landau, Robert C Dennis, st Don Martin, ph Bud Thackery, c Dane Clark. After being tricked into doing robbery, murder ensues.

*Man of Courage* (1943) d Alex Thurn-Taxis, sc Barton MacLane, Arthur St Clare, John Vlahos, st MacLane, Lew Pollack, Herman Ruby, ph Marcel Le Picard, c Barton MacLane.

*Mantrap* (1943) d George Sherman, sc Curt Siodmak, ph William Bradford, c Henry Stephenson.

*The Man Who Cheated Himself* (1951) d Felix Feist, sc Seton I Miller, Philip MacDonald, st Miller, ph Russell Harlan, c Lee J Cobb, John Dall, Jane Wyatt. Wife shoots wealthy husband. Cop/lover covers it up.

*Man With My Face* (1951) d Edward J Montagne, sc Samuel W Taylor, T J McGowan, Vincent Bogert, Montagne, n Taylor, ph Fred Jackman, c Barry Nelson. Doppelgänger Noir. Accountant returns home to find his exact double there.

*Manhandled* (1949) d Lewis R Foster, sc Foster, Whitman Chambers, st L S Goldsmith, ph Ernest Laszlo, c Dorothy Lamour, Dan Duryea, Sterling Hayden. Rich man recounts his nightmare to psychiatrist and the result is death and destruction.

*The Mask of Diljon* (1946) d Lew Landers, sc Arthur St Claire, Griffin Jay, st St Claire, ph Jack Greenhalgh, c Erich Von Stroheim. Former magician uses hypnotism with dire effects.

*The Mask of Dimitrios* (1944) d Jean Negulesco, sc Frank Gruber, n *A Coffin for Dimitrios* Eric Ambler, ph Arthur Edeson, c Sydney Greenstreet, Zachary Scott, Peter Lorre. Mystery writer obsessively investigates mysterious master criminal.

*Miami Expose* (1956) d Fred F Sears, sc Robert E Kent (James B Gordon), ph Benjamin H Kline, c Lee J Cobb, Edward Arnold.

*The Miami Story* (1954) d Fred F Sears, sc st Robert E Kent, ph Henry Freulich, c Barry Sullivan.

*The Midnight Story* (1957) d Joseph Pevney, sc Edwin Blum, John Robinson, ph Russell Metty, c Tony Curtis. Traffic cop gives up job to infiltrate nice Italian family he thinks is responsible for priest's murder.

*Mildred Pierce* (1945) d Michael Curtiz, sc Ranald MacDougall, n James M Cain, ph Ernest Haller, c Joan Crawford. Materialist Noir. Woman under suspicion of murder recounts rise to success to police.

*Million Dollar Pursuit* (1951) d R G Springsteen, sc Albert DeMond, Bradbury Foote, ph Walter Strenge, c Penny Edwards.

*Ministry of Fear* (1944) d Fritz Lang, sc Seton I Miller, n Graham Greene, ph Henry Sharp, c Ray Milland, Dan Duryea. Nightmare Noir. Man just out of mental hospital must make sense out of world of Nazi spies.

*The Missing Juror* (1944) d Budd Boetticher, sc Charles O'Neal, st Leon Abrams, Richard Hill Wilkinson, ph L William O'Connell, c Jim Bannon, George Macready.

*The Mob* (1951) d Robert Parrish, sc William Bowers, n *Waterfront* Ferguson Findley, ph Joseph Walker, c Broderick Crawford. Undercover cops infiltrate waterfront gang.

*Moonrise* (1948) d Frank Borzage, sc Charles Haas, n Theodore Strauss, ph John L Russell, c Dane Clark. The Beast Within Noir. Man who killed in self-defence fears it is his nature to kill.

*Moontide* (1942) d Archie Mayo (& Fritz Lang), sc John O'Hara, n Willard Robertson, ph Charles Clarke, c Jean Gabin, Ida Lupino, Thomas Mitchell, Claude Rains. Seaman falls for suicidal girl. Inspired by French poetic realist films.

*Moss Rose* (1947) d Gregory Ratoff, sc Jules Furthman, Tom Reed, ad Niven Busch, n Joseph Shearing, ph Joe MacDonald, c Peggy Cummins, Victor Mature. Victorian woman blackmails country gent.

*The Mugger* (1958) d William A Berke, sc Henry Kane, n Ed McBain, ph J Bergi Contner, c Kent Smith. The policemen of 87th Precinct hunt a serial mugger who kills a woman.

*Murder by Contract* (1958) d Irving Lerner, sc Ben Simcoe, ph Lucien Ballard, c Vince Edwards. Killer kills, then is killed. 4/5

*Murder is My Beat* (1955) d Edgar G Ulmer, sc Aubrey

Wiseberg, st Wiseberg, Martin Field, ph Harold E Wellman, c Paul Langton, Barbara Payton. On way to prison, woman sees man she was convicted of murdering.

*My Gun is Quick* (1957) d George White, sc Richard Collins, Richard Powell, n Mickey Spillane, ph Harry Neumann, c Robert Bray. Mike Hammer investigates a girl's murder and is on the hunt for a cache of jewels.

*My Name is Julia Ross* (1945) d Joseph H Lewis, sc Muriel Roy Boulton, n *The Woman in Red* Anthony Gilbert, ph Burnett Guffey, c Nina Foch. Nightmare Noir. Woman hired as secretary by old woman and son wakes to be told she is son's mentally unbalanced wife. 5/5

*The Mysterious Mr Valentine* (1946) d Philip Ford, sc Milton Raison, ph Alfred S Keller, c William Henry, Linda Stirling. PI investigates when girl is blackmailed about a hit and run accident.

*Mystery Street* (1950) d John Sturges, sc Sydney Boehm, Richard Brooks, st Leonard Spigelgass, ph John Alton, c Ricardo Montalban. Architect murders cheap woman. Body turns up three months later. Police investigate.

*The Naked Alibi* (1954) d Jerry Hopper, sc Lawrence Roman, s J Robert Bren, Gladys Atwater, ph Russell Metty, c Sterling Hayden, Gloria Grahame. Cop fired for leaning on suspect, then obsessively follows suspect to Mexico.

*The Naked City* (1948) d Jules Dassin, sc Albert Matz, Malvin Wald, st Wald, ph William Daniels, c Barry Fitzgerald, Howard Duff. Docu Noir. Two police detectives track down murderers. 4/5

*The Naked Street* (1955) d Maxwell Shane, sc Shane, Leo Katcher, ph Floyd Crosby, c Farley Granger, Anthony Quinn, Anne Bancroft. Racketeer uses contacts to get his sister's boyfriend out of death row.

*The Narrow Margin* (1952) d Richard Fleischer, sc Earl Felton, st Martin Goldsmith, Jack Leonard, ph George E Diskant, c

Charles McGraw, Marie Windsor. Cop escorts witness cross-country by train. Brilliant twists and turns. 5/5

*New Orleans After Dark* (1958) d John Sledge, sc Frank Phares, ph Willis Winford, c Stacy Harris.

*New York Confidential* (1955) d Russell Rouse, sc Clarence Greene, Rouse, book Jack Lait, Lee Mortimer, ph Edward Fitzgerald, c Broderick Crawford, Richard Conte. Assassin is ordered to kill his best friend.

*Niagara* (1953) d Henry Hathaway, sc Charles Brackett, Walter Reisch, Richard Breen, ph Joe MacDonald, c Marilyn Monroe, Joseph Cotten. Young wife and her lover plans murder of older, mentally unbalanced war vet husband, only to have tables turned. 4/5

*Night and the City* (1950) d Jules Dassin, sc Jo Eisinger, n Gerald Kersh, ph Max Greene, c Richard Widmark, Gene Tierney. Nightmare Noir. Doomed hustler's scheme to control London's wrestling scene goes fatally wrong. 4/5

*Night Editor* (1946) d Henry Levin, sc Hal Smith, radio program Hal Burdick, st Scott Littleton, h Burnett Guffey, c William Gargan. When cop witnesses killing, he can't report it because it would reveal his affair with socialite.

*The Night Has a Thousand Eyes* (1948) d John Farrow, sc Barre Lyndon, Jonathan Latimer, n Cornell Woolrich, ph John F Seitz, c Edward G Robinson. Fate Noir. Fortune-teller discovers he can really see into future, and it's not a good one!

*The Night Holds Terror* (1955) d sc Andrew L Stone, ph Fred Jackman, c Jack Kelley, Vince Edwards, John Cassavetes. Three criminals hold family hostage.

*The Night of the Hunter* (1955) d Charles Laughton, sc James Agee, n Davis Grubb, ph Stanley Cortez, c Robert Mitchum, Lillian Gish. Children go on run, pursued by mad preacher after he kills their mother. 5/5

*The Night Runner* (1957) d Abner Biberman, sc Gene Levitt, st

Owen Cameron, ph George Robinson, c Ray Danton. Psycho/Logical Noir. Mental outpatient pushed over edge by girlfriend's father.

*Night Without Sleep* (1952) d Roy Ward Baker, sc Frank Partos, Elick Moll, n Moll, ph Lucien Ballard, c Linda Darnell, Gary Merrill. Drunk songwriter fears he killed the previous night whilst on binge.

*Nightfall* (1957) d Jacques Tourneur, sc Stirling Silliphant, n David Goodis, ph Burnett Guffey, c Aldo Ray, Brian Keith, Anne Bancroft. Nightmare Noir. Artist is hunted by police for a murder he didn't do, and by robbers for money he doesn't have. 4/5

*Nightmare* (1956) d sc Maxwell Shane, st Cornell Woolrich, ph Joseph Biroc, c Edward G Robinson, Kevin McCarthy. Remake of *Fear in the Night*.

*Nightmare Alley* (1947) d Edmund Goulding, sc Jules Furthman, n William Lindsay Gresham, ph Lee Garmes, c Tyrone Power, Joan Blondell, Coleen Gray. Materialist Noir. Carny makes it big as spiritualist, then sinks to geek. 4/5

*No Escape* (1953, *City on a Hunt*) d sc Charles Bennett, ph Ben Kline, c Lew Ayres, Majorie Steele. Couple accused of murder must find real killer.

*No Man of Her Own* (1950) d Mitchell Leisen, sc Sally Benson, Catherine Turney (& Liesen), n *I Married a Dead Man* Cornell Woolrich, ph Daniel L Fapp, c Barbara Stanwyck. Melodrama Noir. Woman pretends to be someone else so that her baby can have decent life, but...

*No Man's Woman* (1955) d Franklin Adreon, sc John K Butler, Don Martin, ph Bud Thackery, c Marie Windsor. Woman is horrible to everybody and is then killed.

*No Questions Asked* (1951) d Harold F Kress, sc Sidney Sheldon, st Bernard Giler, ph Harold Lipstein, c Barry Sullivan. Lawyer negotiates between criminals and insurance company for return of stolen goods.

*No Way Out* (1950) d Joseph L Mankiewicz, sc Mankiewicz, Lesser Samuels, ph Milton Krasner, c Richard Widmark, Linda Darnell, Sidney Poitier. Hood's brother dies. A black doctor was attending, so hood starts a race riot.

*Nobody Lives Forever* (1946) d Jean Negulesco, sc n W R Burnett, ph Arthur Edeson, c John Garfield. War veteran returns from war to re-establish himself as big-time hustler.

*Nocturne* (1946) d Edwin L Marin, sc Jonathan Latimer, st Frank Fenton, Rowland Brown, ph Harry J Wild, c George Raft. Obsessive cop goes out on a limb to prove songwriter was murdered.

*Nora Prentiss* (1947) d Vincent Sherman, sc Richard Nash, st Paul Webster, Jack Sobell, ph James Wong Howe, c Ann Sheridan. Nightclub singer is with man who faked his own death to be with her.

*Notorious* (1946) d Alfred Hitchcock, sc Ben Hecht, ph Ted Tetzlaff, c Cary Grant, Ingrid Bergman, Claude Rains. Woman goes deep undercover in Nazi spy ring, but loves American agent who sent her there. 5/5

*Obsession* (1949, *The Hidden Room* in US) d Edward Dmytrk, sc pl Alec Coppel, ph C Pennington Richards, c Robert Newton. Tense Noir. Husband plans murder of wife's lover. 4/5

*Odds Against Tomorrow* (1959) d Robert Wise, sc John O Killens (really Abraham Polonsky), Nelson Gidding, n William P McGivern, ph Joseph Brun, c Harry Belafonte, Robert Ryan, Gloria Grahame. Racial Heist Noir. Three losers pull a robery in a small town and it all goes wrong.

*On Dangerous Ground* (1952, *Dark Highway*) d Nicholas Ray, sc A I Bezzerides, ad Bezzerides, Ray, n *Mad With Much Heart* Gerald Butler, ph George E Diskant, c Robert Ryan, Ida Lupino. Brutal city cop finds redemption when eyes opened by blind country woman. 5/5

*Once a Thief* (1950) d W Lee Wilder, sc Richard S Conway, st

Max Colpet, Hans Wilhelm, ph Wiliam Clothier, c June Havoc, Cesar Romero. Down-and-out woman falls for hustler.

*One Way Street* (1950) d Hugo Fregonese, sc Lawrence Kimble, ph Maury Gertsman, c James Mason, Dan Duryea. Doctor steals hood's girl and money then runs to Mexico.

*The Other Woman* (1954) d sc Hugo Haas, ph Eddie Fitzgerald, c Haas. Director is blackmailed by actress.

*Out of the Fog* (1941) d Anatole Litvak, sc Robert Rossen, Jerry Wald, Richard Macaulay, pl Irwin Shaw, ph James Wong Howe, c Ida Lupino, John Garfield. Hood falls for girl when extracting money from father.

*Out of the Past* (1947, *Build My Gallows High*) d Jacques Tourneur, sc n Geoffrey Homes (aka Daniel Mainwaring), ph Nicholas Musuraca, c Robert Mitchum, Jane Greer, Kirk Douglas. PI runs off with femme fatale he's hired to find, and spends rest of his life trying to run away from that mistake. 5/5

*Outrage* (1950) d Ida Lupino, sc Lupino, Malvin Wald, Collier Young, ph Archie Stout, Louis Clyde Stouman, c Mala Powers. Rape and its aftermath.

*Outside the Wall* (1950) d sc Crane Wilbur, st Henry Edward Helseth, ph Irving Glassberg, c Richard Basehart. Ex-con works in sanitarium and gets caught up with criminal patient, wife.

*Over-Exposed* (1956) d Lewis Seiler, sc James Gunn, Gil Orlovitz, st Mary Loos, Richard Sale, ph Henry Freulich, c Cleo Moore, Richard Crenna.

*Panic in the Streets* (1950) d Elia Kazan, sc Richard Murphy, ad Daniel Fuchs, st Edna, Edward Anhalt, ph Joe MacDonald, c Richard Widmark, Barbara Bel Geddes, Jack Palance. Public health doctor tracks down murderer carrying bubonic plague. 5/5

*The Paradine Case* (1947) d Alfred Hitchcock, sc David O

Selznick, ad Alma Reville, n Robert Hichens, ph Lee Garmes, c Gregory Peck, Alida Valli. High-class lawyer falls for beautiful aloof client accused of poisoning her husband. 2/5

*Parole Inc* (1948) d Alfred Zeisler, sc Royal Cole, st Sherman T Lowe, Cole, ph Gilbert Warrenton, c Michael O'Shea. Corruption unveiled in parole system.

*Party Girl* (1958) d Nicholas Ray, sc George Wells, st Leo Katcher, ph Robert Bronner, c Robert Taylor, Cyd Charisse. Crippled lawyer and girl are brought together when gangster threatens them.

*The People Against O'Hara* (1951) d John Sturges, sc John Monks Jr, n Eleazar Lipsky, ph John Alton, c Spencer Tracy. Corrupt drunkard lawyer loses murder case then tries to find killer.

*Pete Kelly's Blues* (1955) d Jack Webb, sc Robert L Breen, ph Harold Rosson, c Jack Webb, Janet Leigh, Edmond O'Brien. Jazzman Pete Kelly caves in to gangster and then decides to fight back.

*Phantom Lady* (1944) d Robert Siodmak, sc Bernard C Shoenfeld, n Cornell Woolrich, ph Woody Bredell, c Franchot Tone, Ella Raines. Secretary tries to save boss from being executed by tracking down real killer of his wife. 5/5

*The Phenix City Story* (1955) d Phil Karlson, sc Crane Wilbur, Daniel Mainwaring, ph Harry Neumann, c John McIntire. Docu Noir. Lawyer back from war finds his home town has become den of corruption.

*Pickup* (1951) d sc Hugo Haas, n *Watchman 47* Joseph Kopta, ph Paul Ivano, c Haas. Woman marries old railroad inspector for money, but he does not have any.

*Pickup on South Street* (1953) d sc Sam Fuller, st Dwight Taylor, ph Joe MacDonald, c Richard Widmark, Jean Peters, Thelma Ritter. Pickpocket accidentally steals microfilm and is caught between spies, police and girl. 5/5

*Pitfall* (1948) d André de Toth, sc Karl Kamb, n Jay Dratler, ph Harry J Wild, c Dick Powell, Lizabeth Scott. Suburban man becomes bored with routine, so gets involved with femme fatale. 4/5

*A Place in the Sun* (1951) d George Stevens, sc Michael Wilson, Harry Brown, n *An American Tragedy* Theodore Dreiser, pl Patrick Kearney, ph William C Mellor, c Montgomery Clift, Elizabeth Taylor, Shelly Winters. Materialist Noir. Man murders to escape lower-class existence.

*Playgirl* (1954) d Joseph Pevney, sc Robert Blees, st Ray Buffum, ph Carl Gutrie, c Shelly Winters, Barry Sullivan. Beautiful country girl comes to the dark city.

*Please Murder Me* (1956) d Peter Godfrey, sc Al C Ward, Donald Hyde, ph Allen Stensvold, c Angela Lansbury, Raymond Burr. Lawyer falls for murderess and goes beyond the law.

*Plunder Road* (1957) d Hubert Cornfield, sc Steven Ritch, Jack Charney, st Ritch, ph Ernest Haller, c Gene Raymond. Heist Noir. Five men rob bullion from train.

*Portland Expose* (1957) d Harold D Schuster, sc Jack DeWitt, ph Carl Berger, c Ed Binns. Tavern owner forced to work with the mob but then rebels when they try to rape his daughter.

*Port of New York* (1949) d Laslo Benedek, sc Ernest Ling, ad Leo Townsend, st Arthur A Ross, Bert Murray, ph George E Diskant, c Scott Brady. Two treasury agents infiltrate waterfront drugs ring.

*Portrait of Jennie* (1948) d William Dieterle, sc Paul Osborn, Peter Berneis, Ben Hecht, David O Selznick, ad Leonardo Bercovici, n Robert Nathan, ph Joseph H August, c Jennifer Jones, Joseph Cotton. A tale of romantic, obsessive love.

*Possessed* (1947) d Curtis Bernhardt, sc Sylvia Richards, Ranald MacDougall, n *One Man's Service* Rita Weiman, ph Joseph Valentine, c Joan Crawford, Van Heflin, Raymond Massey. Psychological Noir. Schizoid woman recounts how her yearning for love led to murder and madness. 5/5

*The Postman Always Rings Twice* (1946) d Tay Garnett, sc Harry Ruskin, Niven Busch, n James M Cain, ph Sidney Wagner, c Lana Turner, John Garfield. Drifter falls for wife of truck café owner, and they murder him. 4/5

*The Pretender* (1947) d W Lee Wilder, sc Don Martin, ph John Alton, c Albert Dekker. Broker hires hood to kill rival but it backfires.

*The Price of Fear* (1956) d Abner Biberman, sc Robert Tallman, st Dick Irving, ph Irving Glassberg, c Merle Oberon. Career woman covers up hit-and-run accident.

*Private Hell 36* (1954) d Don Seigel, sc Collier Young, Ida Lupino, ph Burnett Guffey, c Ida Lupino, Steve Cochran. Two cops take suitcase of money.

*The Prowler* (1951) d Joseph Losey, sc Hugo Butler, st Robert Thoeren, Hans Wilhelm, ph Arthur Miller, c Van Heflin, Evelyn Keyes. Materialist Noir. Cop seduces suburban housewife then plots to kill her husband. 4/5

*The Pusher* (1960) d Gene Milford, sc Harold Robbins, n Ed McBain, ph Arthur J Ornitz, c Kathy Caryle, Robert Lansing. Steve Carella of the 87th Precinct investigates the murder of a heroin addict and discovers a connection to his fiancée.

*Pushover* (1954) d Richard Quine, sc Roy Huggins, n *The Night Watcher* Thomas Walsh, *Rafferty* William S Ballinger, ph Lester H White, c Fred MacMurray, Kim Novak. Police detective falls for woman under surveillance, then plots murder.

*Queen Bee* (1955) d sc Ranald MacDougall, n Edna Lee, ph Charles Lang, c Joan Crawford, Barry Sullivan.

*Quicksand* (1950) d Irving Pichel, sc Robert Smith, ph Lionel Lindon, c Mickey Rooney. Garage mechanic slides into criminal life.

*Race Street* (1948) d Edwin L Marin, sc Martin Rackin, st

Maurice Davis, ph J Roy Hunt, c George Raft, William Bendix. Bookie avenges murder of friend.

*The Racket* (1951) d John Cromwell, sc William Wister Haines, W R Burnett, pl Bartlett Cormack, ph George E Diskant, c Robert Mitchum, Lizabeth Scott, Robert Ryan. Policeman and gangster vie for power in corrupt city. Remake of 1928 film.

*Rage in Heaven* (1941) d W S Van Dyke, sc Christopher Isherwood, Robert Thoeren, n James Hilton, ph Oliver T Marsh, c Robert Montgomery, Ingrid Bergman. Secretary marries mentally unbalanced industrialist.

*The Raging Tide* (1951) d George Sherman, sc n *Fiddler's Green* Ernest K Gann, ph Russell Metty, c Richard Conte, Shelly Winters. Killer works on fishing boat whilst trapped in San Francisco.

*Railroaded* (1947) d Anthony Mann, sc John C Higgins, st Gertrude Walker, ph Guy Roe, c John Ireland. Police detectives out to prove girlfriend's brother is not killer.

*Raw Deal* (1948) d Anthony Mann, sc Leopold Atlas, John C Higgins, st Arnold B Armstrong, Audrey Ashley, ph John Alton, c Dennis O'Keefe, Clair Trevor. On the run from prison, seeking revenge on gangster who framed him, con is caught between two women. 5/5

*Rebecca* (1940) d Alfred Hitchcock, sc Robert E Sherwood, Joan Harrison, n Daphne du Maurier, ph George Barnes, c Laurence Olivier, Joan Fontaine. Gothic Noir. Timid woman marries nobleman haunted by first wife. 4/5

*The Reckless Moment* (1949) d Max Ophüls, sc Henry Garson, Robert W Soderberg, ad Mel Dinelli, Robert E Kent, n *The Blank Wall* Elizabeth Sanxay Holding, ph Burnett Guffey, c James Mason, Joan Bennett. Class Noir. Woman fights to protect family from shame.

*The Red House* (1947) d sc Delmar Daves, n George Agnew Chamberlain, ph Bert Glennon, c Edward G Robinson.

Psychological Noir. Farmer protects secret of house on his land.

*Red Light* (1950) d Roy Del Ruth, sc George Callahan, ph Bert Glennon, c George Raft. When priest is murdered, brother takes revenge.

*Red Menace* (1949) d R G Springsteen, sc Albert DeMond, Gerald Geraghty, st DeMond, ph John MacBurnie, c Robert Rockwell. Man joins Communist Party and falls in love with instructor, but are hunted down when they try to leave.

*Repeat Performance* (1947) d Alfred L Werker, sc Walter Bullock, n William O'Farrell, ph L William O'Connell, c Louis Hayward, Joan Leslie, Richard Basehart. An actress kills her cheating husband and is then given the chance to relive the past year.

*Revolt in the Big House* (1958) d R G Springsteen, sc Daniel James, Eugene Lourié, ph William Margulies, c Gene Evans, Robert Blake, Timothy Carey. Big time criminal stages riot as a diversion for an escape plan.

*Ride the Pink Horse* (1947) d Robert Montgomery, sc Ben Hecht, Charles Lederer, n Dorothy B Hughes, ph Russell Metty, c Robert Montgomery. War vet goes to Mexico to exact revenge.

*Riffraff* (1947) d Ted Tetzlaff, sc Martin Rackin, ph George E Diskant, c Pat O'Brien, Walter Slezak. PI/con man Dan Hammer has oil information for sale in Panama.

*Riot in Cell Block 11* (1954) d Don Seigel, sc Richard Collins, ph Russell Harlan, c Neville Brand. Prison inmates are pushed too far.

*Road House* (1948) d Jean Negulesco, sc Edward Chodorov, st Margaret Gruen, Oscar Saul, ph Joseph La Shelle, c Ida Lupino, Cornel Wilde, Richard Widmark. Melodrama Noir. Roadhouse owner frames manager so that he can get girl singer. 3/5

*Roadblock* (1951) d Harold Daniels, sc Steve Fisher, George

Bricker, st Richard Landau, Geoffrey Homes (Daniel Mainwaring), ph Nicholas Musuraca, c Charles McGraw. Insurance investigator does robbery to please greedy girlfriend.

*Rogue Cop* (1954) d Roy Rowland, sc Sydney Boehm, n William P McGivern, ph John F Seitz, c Robert Taylor, Janet Leigh, George Raft. Cop seeks revenge for murdered brother.

*Rope of Sand* (1949) d William Dieterle, sc Walter Doniger, ph Charles B Lang, c Burt Lancaster, Paul Henried, Claude Rains, Peter Lorre. Man goes to North Africa to rob jewels he was wrongly accused of stealing.

*Ruby Gentry* (1952) d King Vidor, sc Sylvia Richards, st Arthur Fitz-Richard, ph Russell Harlan, c Jennifer Jones, Charlton Heston. Melodrama Noir. Seedy girl marries for money when true love rejects her.

*Ruthless* (1948) d Edgar G Ulmer, sc Lauren, Gordon Kahn, n *Prelude to Night* Dayton Stoddart, ph Bert Glennon, c Zachary Scott, Louis Hayward, Sydney Greenstreet. Citizen Kane Noir. Man tells story of childhood friend who became powerful man.

*Saigon* (1948) d Leslie Fenton, sc Arthur Sheekman, P J Wolfson, st Julian Zimet, ph John F Seitz, c Alan Ladd, Veronica Lake. Man is going to die so his friends make sure he has a lifetime of experiences.

*San Quentin* (1946) d Gordon Douglas, sc Howard J Green, Lawrence Kimble, Marton Mooney, Arthur A Ross, ph Frank Redamn, c Lawrence Tierney, Barton MacLane. Ex-con hunts down his old friend.

*Scandal Sheet* (1952) d Phil Karlson, sc Ted Sherdeman, Eugene Ling, James Poe, n *The Dark Page* Samuel Fuller, ph Burnett Guffey, c John Derek, Donna Reed, Broderick Crawford. Newspaper editor murders wife and his reporter investigates why.

*The Scarf* (1951) d sc E A Dupont, n *The Dungeon* I G Goldsmith, Edwin Rolfe (aka Dupont), ph Franz Planer, c John Ireland, Mercedes McCambridge. Madman escapes from asylum and tries to convince people he is not a murderer.

*The Scarlet Hour* (1956) d Michael Curtiz, sc John Meredyth Lucas, Frank Tashlin, Alford Van Ronkel, st The Kiss off Tashlin, ph Lionel Lindon, c Carol Ohmart, Tom Tryon. Lovers hijack a jewel thief gang to finance elopement.

*Scarlet Street* (1945) d Fritz Lang, sc Dudley Nichols, n pl *La Chienne* Georges de la Fouchardiere, ph Milton Krasner, John P Fulton, c Edward G Robinson, Joan Bennett, Dan Duryea. Nightmare Noir. Man hooked by femme fatale and her partner. Remake of Jean Renoir's 1931 film *La Chienne*. 4/5

*Scene of the Crime* (1949) d Roy Rowland, sc Charles Schnee, st John Bartlow Martin, ph Paul C Vogel, c Van Johnson. Cop investigates murder of partner who may have been crooked.

*Screaming Mimi* (1958) d Gerd Oswald, sc Robert Blees, n Fredric Brown, ph Burnett Guffey, c Ania Ekberg. Series of murders linked to mad dancer and her manager.

*Sealed Lips* (1942) d sc st *Beyond the Law* George Waggner, ph Stanley Cortez, c William Gargan. Detective thinks imprisoned man is innocent.

*Second Chance* (1953) d Rudolph Maté, sc Sydney Boehm, Oscar Millard, Robert Presnell Sr, st D M Marshman Jr, ph William E Snyder, c Robert Mitchum, Linda Darnell, Jack Palance. Woman hides from mob boyfriend in Mexico and wants protection from an ex-boxer.

*The Second Woman* (1951) d James V Kern, sc Robert Smith, Mort Briskin, ph Hal Mohr, c Robert Young. Architect goes mad from feelings of guilt over girlfriend's death.

*Secret Behind the Door* (1948) d Fritz Lang, sc Sylvia Richards, st Rufus King, ph Stanley Cortez, c Joan Bennett, Michael Redgrave. Timid woman marries mentally unbalanced architect who may have killed first wife. 3/5

*The Secret Fury* (1950) d Mel Ferrer, sc Lionel Houser, st Jack R Leonard, James O'Hanlon, ph Leo Tover, c Claudette Colbert, Robert Ryan. Bride-to-be murders and goes to asylum.

*The Sellout* (1952) d Gerald Mayer, sc Charles Palmer, st Matthew Rapf, ph Paul C Vogel, c Walter Pidgeon, John Hodiak, Audrey Totter. Newspaper editor versus corrupt sheriff.

*The Set-Up* (1949) d Robert Wise, sc Art Cohn, poem Joseph Moncure March, ph Milton Krasner, c Robert Ryan, Audrey Totter. Boxer refuses to take a dive. Filmed in real time. Tense. 5/5

*The Seventh Victim* (1943) d Mark Robson, sc Charles O'Neal, DeWitt Bodeen, ph Nicholas Musuraca, c Tom Conwat, Kim Hunter. Nightmare Noir. Woman spends night searching for sister, escaped from secret sect.

*Shack Out on 101* (1955) d Edward Dein, sc st Edward Dein, Mildred Dein, ph Floyd Crosby, c Terry Moore, Frank Lovejoy, Lee Marvin. Sexual chemistry and atomic spies on the menu.

*Shadowed* (1946) d John Sturges, sc Brenda Weisberg, st Julian Harmon, ph Henry Freulich, c Lloyd Corrigan. Man accidentally discovers a murder on the golf course and is dragged into a world of escalating terror.

*Shadow of a Doubt* (1943) d Alfred Hitchcock, sc Thornton Wilder, Sally Benson, Alma Reville, st Gordon McDonnell, ph Joseph Valentine, c Teresa Wright, Joseph Cotten. Small Town Noir. Girl fears visiting uncle may be murderer. 5/5

*Shadow of a Woman* (1946) d Joseph Santley, sc Whitman Chambers, Graham Baker, n *He Fell Down Dead* Virginia Perdue, ph Bert Glennon, c Helmut Dantine, Andrea King.

Highly strung woman marries mysterious man.

*Shadow of Fear* (1956, *Before I Wake*) d Albert S Rogell, sc Robert Westerby, n *Before I Wake* Hal Debrett, ph Jack Asher, c Mona Freeman. After her father's death, woman realises her stepmother killed him, and she's next!

*Shadow on the Wall* (1950) d Pat Jackson, sc William Ludwig, n *Devil in the Doll's House* Hannah Lees, Lawrence P Bachman, ph Ray June, c Ann Sothern, Zachary Scott. Psychiatrist tries to unlock mind of girl who witnessed murder.

*Shadow on the Window* (1957) d William Asher, sc Leo Townsend, David P Harmon, st John, Ward Hawkins, ph Kit Carson, c Phil Carey. Three burglars kill owner of farmhouse and hold secretary hostage.

*Shakedown* (1950) d Joseph Pevney, sc Alfred Lewis Levitt, Martin Goldsmith, st Nat Dallinger, Don Martin, ph Irving Glassberg, c Howard Duff, Brian Donlevy, Lawrence Tierney. Photographer gets involved with criminals.

*The Shanghai Gesture* (1941) d Josef von Sternberg, sc von Sternberg, Karl Vollmoeller, Geza Herczeg, Jules Furthman, pl John Colton, ph Paul Ivano, c Gene Tierney, Walter Huston, Victor Mature. British financier discovers daughter is victim of Shanghai decadence.

*Shed No Tears* (1948) d Jean Yarbrough, sc Brown Holmes, Virginia Cook, n Don Martin, ph Frank Redman, c Wallace Ford. Man fakes death, but wife plans to double-cross him and collect insurance.

*Shield for Murder* (1954) d Edmond O'Brien, Howard W Koch, sc Richard Alen Simmons, John C Higgins, ad Simmons, n William P McGivern, ph Gordon Avil, c Edmond O'Brien. Corrupt cop murders bookie when he doesn't hand over pay-off, and convinces bosses it's a legit killing.

*Shock* (1946) d Alfred Werker, sc Eugene Ling, st Albert DeMond, ph Glen MacWilliams, c Vincent Price.

Psychiatrist who committed murder treats witness suffering from shock.

*Shockproof* (1949) d Douglas Sirk, sc Helen Deutsch, Samuel Fuller, st Fuller, ph Charles Lawton, c Cornel Wilde, Patricia Knight. Parole officer falls for parolee and slides into life of crime. 4/5

*Shoot to Kill* (1947) d William Berke, sc Edwin Westrate, ph Benjamin Kline, c Russell Wade. Crooked District Attorney falls for wife of man he framed.

*Short Cut to Hell* (1957) d James Cagney, sc Ted Berkman, Ralph Blau, W R Burnett, n *This Gun for Hire* Graham Greene, ph Haskell Boggs, c Robert Ivers. Professional assassin is double-crossed.

*Side Street* (1950) d Anthony Mann, sc Sydney Boehm, ph Joseph Ruttenberg, c Farley Granger, Cathy O'Donnell. Nightmare Noir. Postman accidentally steals mail and is propelled into nightmare criminal world.

*The Sign of the Ram* (1948) d John Sturges, sc Charles Bennett, n Margaret Ferguson, ph Burnett Guffey, c Susan Peters, Alexander Knox. Melodrama Noir. Crippled woman rules people around her.

*Singapore* (1947) d John Brahm, sc Seton I Miller, Robert Teoren, st Miller, ph Maury Gertsman, c Fred MacMurray, Ava Gardner. Man returns to Singapore to recover pearls he hid during combat and bumps into his 'dead' girlfriend.

*Sirocco* (1951) d Curtis Bernhardt, sc A I Bezzerides, Hans Jacoby, n Joseph Kessel, ph Burnett Guffey, c Humphrey Bogart. Mercenary gets caught in rebellion.

*Sleep, My Love* (1948) d Douglas Sirk, sc Claire McKelway, Leo Rosten, n Rosten, ph Joseph Valentine, c Claudette Colbert, Robert Cummings. Man tries to drive wife to suicide.

*The Sleeping City* (1950) d George Sherman, sc Jo Eisinger, ph William Miller, c Richard Conte, Coleen Gray. Hospital Noir. Cop goes undercover in hospital.

*The Sleeping Tiger* (1954) d Victor Hanbury (aka Joseph Losey), sc Harold Buchman, Carl Foreman, n Maurice Moisewisch, ph Harry Waxman, c Dirk Bogarde. Psychiatrist brings home criminal to study, arousing interest of bored wife. 3/5

*Slightly Scarlet* (1956) d Allan Dwan, sc Robert Blees, n *Love's Lovely Counterfeit* James M Cain, ph John Alton, c John Payne. Good/bad criminal takes over city and falls for good/bad sisters.

*Smart Girls Don't Talk* (1948) d Richard L Bare, sc William Sackheim, ph Ted D McCord, c Virginia Mayo, Bruce Bennett.

*Smash-Up, The Story of a Woman* (1947) d Stuart Heisler, sc John Howard Lawson, st Dorothy Parker, Frank Cavett, ph Stanley Cortez, c Susan Hayward. A woman becomes an alcoholic.

*The Sniper* (1952) d Edward Dmytryk, sc Harry Brown, st Edna, Edward Anhalt, ph Burnett Guffey, c Adolphe Menjou, Arthur Franz. Psychopath is compelled to shoot women from rooftops. 5/5

*So Dark the Night* (1946) d Joseph H Lewis, sc Martin Berkeley, Dwight Babcock, st Aubrey Wisberg, ph Burnett Guffey, c Steven Geray. Parisian detective falls in love whilst on vacation – his love becomes the first victim in a series of murders.

*So Evil My Love* (1949) d Lewis Allen, sc Leonard Spigelgass, Ronald Miller, n *For Her to See* Joseph Shearing, ph Max Greene, c Ann Todd, Ray Milland. Timid Victorian woman falls for artist, enters dark world and by the end becomes a cold-blooded murderess.

*Somewhere in the Night* (1946) d Joseph L Mankiewicz, sc Mankiewicz, Howard Dimsdale, ad Lee Strasberg, st Martin Borowsky, ph Norbert Brodine, c John Hodiak. Amnesic war verteran gets involved with Nazi treasure whilst searching for past.

*Sorry, Wrong Number* (1948) d Anatole Litvak, sc radio pl Lucille Fletcher, ph Sol Polito, c Barbara Stanwyck, Burt Lancaster. Bedridden heiress hears murder plan over phone, investigates and finds out she is the victim. 4/5

*The Sound of Fury* (1950, *Try and Get Me*) d Cyril Endfield, sc n *The Condemned* Jo Pagano, ph Guy Roe, c Frank Lovejoy, Lloyd Bridges. After befriending small-time hood, war vet sucked into spiralling life of crime.

*Southside 1-1000* (1950) d Boris Ingster, sc Leo Townsend, Ingster, st Milton M Raison, Bert C Brown, ph Russell Harlan, c Don DeFore. Treasury agent goes undercover to find counterfeiters.

*Specter of the Rose* (1946) d sc Ben Hecht, ph Lee Garmes, c Judith Anderson. Ballet dancer is going mad.

*Spellbound* (1945) d Alfred Hitchcock, sc Ben Hecht, ad Angus MacPhail, n *The House of Dr Edwardes* Francis Breeding, ph George Barnes, c Ingrid Bergman, Gregory Peck. Female psychiatrist falls for impostor who takes over asylum and may be murderer. 2/5

*The Spider* (1945) d Robert D Webb, sc Jo Eisinger, W Scott Darling, st Charles Fulton Oursler, Lowell Brentano, ph Glen MacWilliams, c Richard Conte. Private eye hunted by both killer and police.

*Split Second* (1953) d Dick Powell, sc William Bowers, Irving Wallace, st Chester Erskine, Wallace, ph Nicholas Musuraca, c Stephen McNally, Alexis Smith. Killer escapes prison and takes hostages to a desert ghost town, with an atom bomb due to go off the next day!

*The Spiral Staircase* (1946) d Robert Siodmak, sc Mel Dinelli, n *Some Must Watch* Ethel Lina White, ph Nicholas Musuraca, c Dorothy McGuire. Psychokiller preys on handicapped women. 4/5

*Stage Fright* (1950) d Alfred Hitchcock, sc Whitfield Cook, ad Alma Reville, st Selwyn Jepson, ph Wilkie Cooper, c

Marlene Dietrich, Jane Wyman, Richard Todd. Young woman tries to prove friend innocent of murder, and puts herself in jeopardy. 2/5

*The Steel Jungle* (1956) d sc Walter Doniger, ph J Peverell Marley, c Perry Lopez. In prison, man persuaded to betray gangster.

*The Steel Trap* (1952) d sc Andrew L Stone, ph Ernest Laszlo, c Joseph Cotten, Teresa Wright. Banker tries to rob vault.

*Step by Step* (1946) d Phil Rosen, sc Stuart Palmer, st George Callahan, ph Frank Redman, c Lawrence Tierney. War veteran and woman get caught up in Nazi spy plot.

*Step Down to Terror* (1959) d Harry Keller, sc Mel Dinelli, Czenzi Ormonde, Chris Cooper, st Gordon McDonell, ph Russell Metty, c Charles Drake. Essentially a remake of *Shadow of a Doubt*, with son returning home instead of uncle.

*Storm Fear* (1956) d Cornel Wilde, sc Horton Foote, n Clinton Seeley, ph Joseph La Shelle, c Cornel Wilde, Jean Wallace, Dan Duryea. Bank robber on run hides out in brother's farmhouse to heal wounds, igniting sibling tensions.

*Storm Warning* (1950) d Stuart Heisler, sc Daniel Fuchs, Richard Brooks, st Fuchs, ph Eugene Ritchie, c Ginger Rogers, Ronald Reagan, Doris Day. Woman visits home town to see sister and gets caught up in Ku Klux Klan terrorism.

*The Story of Molly X* (1949) d sc Crane Wilbur, ph Irving Glassberg, c June Havoc. Tough woman runs robbery gang.

*The Strange Affair of Uncle Harry* (1945, *Uncle Harry!*) d Robert Siodmak, sc Stephen Longstreet, ad Keith Winter, pl Thomas Job, ph Paul Ivano, c George Sanders. Bachelor's marriage plans hindered by sisters he lives with.

*Strange Bargain* (1949) d Will Price, sc Lillie Hayward, st J H Wallis, ph Harry Wild, c Martha Scott. Bookkeeper helps wealthy man carry out suicide plan.

*Strange Fascination* (1952) d sc Hugo Haas, ph Paul Ivano, c Cleo Moore, Hugo Haas. Pianist's life ruined by femme fatale.

*Strange Illusion* (1945) d Edgar G Ulmer, sc Adele Commandini, st Fritz Rotter, ph Philip Tannura, c James Lydon. Boy thinks father killed by mother's lover.

*Strange Impersonation* (1946) d Anthony Mann, sc Mindret Lord, st Anne Wigton, Louis Herman, ph Robert W Pittack, c Brenda Marshall. Disfigured woman has plastic surgery, then takes place of dead blackmailer.

*The Strange Love of Martha Ivers* (1946) d Lewis Milestone, sc Robert Rossen, st Jack Patrick, ph Victor Milner, c Barbara Stanwyck, Van Heflin, Lizabeth Scott, Kirk Douglas. Melodrama Noir. Back in home town man falls for girl and meets arguing couple with whom he shares secret past.

*Strange Triangle* (1946, *Strange Alibi*) d Ray McCarey, sc Mortimer Braus, ad Charles G Booth, st Jack Andrews, ph Harry Jackson, c Signe Hasso, Preston Foster. Bank investigator joins couple in embezzlement plan, which leads to murder.

*The Strange Woman* (1946) d Edgar G Ulmer, sc Herb Meadow, n Ben Ames Williams, ph Lucien Andriot, c Hedy Lamarr, George Sanders. Femme Fatale Noir. Woman destroys men on way to top of society.

*The Stranger* (1946) d Orson Welles, sc Anthony Veiller (& Orson Welles, John Huston), st Victor Trivas, ph Russell Metty, c Edward G Robinson, Loretta Young, Orson Welles. A Nazi war criminal is hunted down in a small town.

*Stranger on the Prowl* (1953) d Andrea Forzano (aka Joseph Losey), sc Ben Barzman, st Noel Calef, ph Henri Alekan, c Paul Muni. Hobo kills by accident and while on run is joined by young man.

*The Stranger on the Third Floor* (1940) d Boris Ingster, sc Frank Partos (& Nathanael West), ph Nicholas Musuraca, c Peter

Lorre. Newspaper reporter's evidence convicts murderer, but he doubts his own evidence.

*Strangers in the Night* (1944) d Anthony Mann, sc Bryant Ford, Paul Gangelin, st Philip MacDonald, ph Reggie Lanning, c William Terry. Disturbed woman invents daughter and then must explain when pen-pal soldier returns from war front.

*Strangers on a Train* (1951) d Alfred Hitchcock, sc Raymond Chandler, Czenzi Ormonde, ad Whitfield Cook, n Patricia Highsmith, ph Robert Burks, c Farley Granger, Robert Walker. On train, one man suggests to another that they swap murders. 4/5

*Street of Chance* (1942) d Jack Hively, sc Garrett Fort, n *The Black Curtain* Cornell Woolrich, ph Theodor Sparkul, c Burgess Meredith, Claire Trevor. First Amnesia Noir. Man has accident and returns home to find that he has been missing for a year.

*The Street With No Name* (1948) d William Keighley, sc Harry Kleiner, ph Joe MacDonald, c Mark Stevens, Richard Widmark. Docu Noir. FBI agent goes undercover to catch robbers. 4/5

*The Strip* (1951) d Leslie Kardos, sc Allen Rivkin, ph Robert Surtees, c Mickey Rooney, Sally Forrest. Jazz musician and actress get mixed up in criminal world.

*Sudden Danger* (1955) d Hubert Cornfield, sc Dan, Ellwood Ullman, ph Ellsworth Fredricks, c Bill Elliott. Blind man regains sight then tries to prove himself innocent of murder.

*Sudden Fear* (1952) d David Miller, sc Lenore Coffee, Robert Smith, n Edna Sherry, ph Charles B Lang, c Joan Crawford, Jack Palance, Gloria Grahame. Melodrama Noir. Playwright finds out her husband wants to kill her.

*Suddenly* (1954) d Lewis Allen, sc Richard Sale, ph Charles Clarke, c Frank Sinatra, Sterling Hayden. Planning to assassinate the President, three gunmen hold family hostage. Sinatra excellent as psychopath. 4/5

*The Sun Sets at Dawn* (1950) d sc st Paul H Sloane, ph Lionel Lindon, c Philip Shawn. Innocent man on death row tells his story in flashbacks.

*Sunset Boulevard* (1950) d Billy Wilder, sc Charles Brackett, Wilder, D M Marshman Jr, ph John F Seitz, c William Holden, Gloria Swanson. Screenwriter tells of his mercenary involvement with ageing silent film star. 5/5

*The Suspect* (1945) d Robert Siodmak, sc Bertram Millhouser, ad Arthur T Horman, n *This Way Out* James Ronald, ph Paul Ivano, c Charles Laughton, Ella Raines. Victorian middle-aged man is driven to murder by wife whilst dreaming of new life with beautiful girl.

*Suspense* (1946) d Frank Tuttle, sc Phillip Yordan, ph Karl Struss, c Barry Sullivan. Promoter's affair with ice star leads to murder.

*Suspicion* (1941) d Alfred Hitchcock, sc Samson Raphaelson, Joan Harrison, Alma Reville, n *Before the Fact* Francis Iles, ph Harry Stradling, c Joan Fontaine, Cary Grant. Timid woman suspects new husband wants to murder her. 4/5

*Sweet Smell of Success* (1957) d Alexander MacKendrick, sc Clifford Odets, st ad Ernest Lehman, ph James Wong Howe, c Burt Lancaster, Tony Curtis. Acidic newspaper columnist wants to protect his sister so smears her jazz musician boyfriend. 5/5

*The System* (1953) d Lewis Seiler, sc Jo Eisinger, st Edith, Samuel Grafton, ph Edwin Dupar, c Frank Lovejoy. Bookie discovers he is in the wrong business if he wants to remain honest.

*T-Men* (1948) d Anthony Mann, sc John C Higgins (& Mann), st Virginnia Kellogg, ph John Alton, c Dennis O'Keefe. Treasury agents go undercover to catch counterfeiters. 4/5

*Take One False Step* (1949) d Chester Erskine, sc Irwin Shaw, Erskine, st Irwin, David Shaw, ph Franz Planer, c Wiliam Powell, Shelley Winters. Married professor on the run for murder of old girlfriend.

*Talk About a Stranger* (1952) d David Bradley, sc Margaret Fitts, st Charlotte Armstrong, ph John Alton, c George Murphy. Boy is sure neighbour has poisoned his dog.

*The Tall Target* (1951) d Anthony Mann, sc Art Cohn, st Daniel Mainwaring (Geoffrey Homes), George Worthing Yates, ph Paul C Vogel, c Dick Powell. Trying to stop an assassination attempt on Abe Lincoln whilst travelling by train.

*The Tattered Dress* (1957) d Jack Arnold, sc George Zuckerman, ph Carl E Guthrie, c Jeff Chandler, Jeanne Crain. Brilliant lawyer visits desert resort to defend unpopular man, and after winning finds himself charged with bribery.

*The Tattooed Stranger* (1950) d Edward J Montagne, sc Phil Reisman Jr, ph William Steiner, c John Miles. Rookie detective leads investigation into series of murders.

*Teenage Doll* (1957) d Roger Corman, sc Charles B Griffith, ph Floyd Crosby, c June Kenney. Behind the scenes of girl gang The Black Widows.

*Temptation* (1946) d Irving Pichel, sc Robert Thoeren, n *Bella Donna* Robert Hitchens, pl James Bernard Fagen, ph Lucien Ballard, c Merle Oberon. Victorian femme fatale in Egypt.

*Tension* (1950) d John Berry, sc Allen Rivkin, st John Klorer, ph Harry Stradling, c Richard Basehart, Audrey Totter. Timid pharmacist plans to murder adulterous wife. 4/5

*Terror at Midnight* (1956) d Franklin Adreon, sc John K Butler, st Butler, Irving Shulman, ph Bud Thackery, c Scott Brady. Cop's girl is blackmailed.

*They Drive by Night* (1940) d Raoul Walsh, sc Jerry Wald, Richard Macaulay, n *The Long Haul* A I Bezzerides, ph Arthur Edeson, c George Raft, Humphrey Bogart, Ida Lupino. Truck drivers fight to stay in business and alive. 4/5

*They Live by Night* (1949, *The Twisted Road* in UK) d Nicholas Ray, sc Charles Schnee, ad Ray, n *Thieves Like Us* Edward Anderson, ph George E Diskant, c Cathy O'Donnell, Farley Granger. Young robber falls for innocent girl and they cannot find a peaceful life with each other. 4/5

*They Made Me a Killer* (1946) d William C Thomas, sc Daniel Mainwaring (Geoffrey Homes), Winston Miller, Kae Salkow, ph Fred Jackman Jr, c.

*They Won't Believe Me* (1947) d Irving Pichel, sc Jonathan Latimer, st Gordon McDonell, ph Harry J Wild, c Robert Young, Susan Hayward, Jane Greer. Promiscuous man ends up charged with murder.

*The Thief* (1952) d Russell Rouse, sc Clarence Greene, Rouse, ph Sam Leavitt, c Ray Milland. Dialogue-free story of scientist on run when he sells secrets to Communists.

*Thieves' Highway* (1949) d Jules Dassin, sc n *Thieves' Market* A I Bezzerides, ph Norbert Brodine, c Richard Conte. War vet truck driver fights crooked fruit wholesaler. 4/5

*The Thirteenth Letter* (1951) d Otto Preminger, sc Howard Koch, st sc Louis Chavance, ph Joseph La Shelle, c Linda Darnell, Charles Boyer. Remake of Henri-Georges Clouzot's *Le Corbeau* (1943) about poison pen letters unsettling a Canadian village.

*This Gun for Hire* (1942) d Frank Tuttle, sc Albert Maltz, W R Burnett, n Graham Greene, ph John F Seitz, c Alan Ladd, Veronica Lake. When assassin is paid with 'hot' bills, he goes after boss whilst being pursued by the law.

*This Side of the Law* (1950) d Richard Bare, sc Russell Hughes, st Richard Sale, ph Carl Guthrie, c Viveca Lindfors. Corrupt lawyer hires man to impersonate rich client.

*This Woman is Dangerous* (1952) d Felix Feist, sc Geoffrey Homes (aka Daniel Mainwaring), George Worthing Yates, st Bernard Girard, ph Ted McCord, c Joan Crawford. Female criminal falls for doctor trying to restore her sight.

*The Threat* (1949) d Felix Feist, sc Hugh King, Dick Irving, st King, ph Harry Wild, c Michael O'Shea. Killer escapes prison and holds hostage the three people who helped put him away.

*Three Bad Sisters* (1956) d Gilbert Kay, sc Gerlad Drayson Adams, st Devery Freeman, ph Lester Shorr, c Marla English, Kathleen Hughes, Sara Shane. Three sisters inherit fortune but one doesn't want to share.

*Three Steps North* (1951) d W Lee Wilder, sc Lester Fuller, st Robert Harari, ph Aldo Giordano, c Lloyd Bridges. After burying treasure in Italy during the war, man goes back to collect it.

*Three Strangers* (1946) d Jean Negulesco, sc John Huston, Howard Koch, ph Arthur Edeson, c Sydney Greenstreet, Geraldine Fitzgerald, Peter Lorre. Three strangers test luck based on Chinese superstition and suffer consequences.

*Thunder Road* (1958) d Arthur Ripley, sc James Atlee Phillips, Walter Wise, st Robert Mitchum, ph David Ettenson, Alan Stensvold, c Robert Mitchum. Korean war vet takes over family moonshine business but has to fight off the law and gangster rivals.

*Tight Spot* (1955) d Phil Karlson, sc William Bowers, n Leonard Kantor, ph Burnett Guffey, c Ginger Rogers, Edward G Robinson. Convicted woman guarded by cop so she can be a witness against her former boyfriend.

*Timetable* (1956) d Mark Stevens, sc Aben Kandel, st Robert Angus, ph Charles Van Enger, c Mark Stevens. Train robbery is investigated by insurance man who carried it out.

*To Have and to Have Not* (1944) d Howard Hawks, sc Jules Furthman, William Faulkner, n Ernest Hemingway, ph Sidney Hickox, c Humphrey Bogart, Lauren Bacall. Sailor hires out boat to ferry a fugitive from the Nazis. 3/5

*To the Ends of the Earth* (1948) d Robert Stevenson, sc Jay Richard Kennedy, ph Burnett Guffey, c Dick Powell. Government man hunts drug ring.

*Tomorrow is Another Day* (1951) d Felix Feist, sc Art Cohn, Guy Endore, ph Robert Burks, c Steve Cochran. Ex-con runs away with girlfriend after killing her old boyfriend.

*Tomorrow is Forever* (1946) d Irving Pichel, sc Lenore Coffee, n Gwen Bristow, ph Joseph Valentine, c Claudette Colbert, Orson Welles.

*Too Late for Tears* (1949) d Byron Haskin, sc n Roy Huggins, ph William Mellor, c Lizabeth Scott, Dan Duryea. When bag of stolen money drops into their car, married couple begin to have problems. Wife is transformed by greed.

*Touch of Evil* (1958) d sc Orson Welles, n *Badge of Evil* Whit Masterson, ph Russell Metty, c Charlton Heston, Janet Leigh, Orson Welles, Joseph Calleia. Mexican drugs investigator clashes with corrupt American cop in border town after millionaire is blown up. Also available as Director's Cut. 5/5

*The Trap* (1959) d Norman Panama, sc Panama, Richard Alan Simmons, ph Daniel Fapp, c Richard Widmark.

*Trapped* (1949) d Richard Fleischer, sc Earl Felton, George Zuckerman, ph Guy Roe, c Lloyd Bridges. Treasury agents let prisoner escape to follow him to gang.

*The Treasure of the Sierra Madre* (1948) d sc John Huston, n B Traven, ph Ted D McCord, c Humphrey Bogart, Walter Huston, Tim Holt. Three men find gold and greed gets the better of them. 5/5

*The Turning Point* (1952) d William Dieterle, sc Warren Duff, st Horace McCoy, ph Lionel Lindon, c William Holden, Edmond O'Brien. Reporter helps crime committee and finds father of chairman in the pay of the mob.

*Twist of Fate* (1954, *The Beautiful Stranger*) d David Miller, sc Robert Westerby, Carl Nystrom, st Rip Von Ronkel, David Miller, ph Robert Day, Ted Scaife, c Ginger Rogers. Actress finds out fiancé is violent criminal.

*The Two Mrs Carrolls* (1947) d Peter Godfrey, sc Thomas Job, pl Martin Vale, ph Peverell Marley, c Humphrey Bogart, Barbara Stanwyck. When artist finishes wife's portrait he intends to finish her, as he did with his first wife.

*Two o'Clock Courage* (1945) d Anthony Mann, sc Robert E Kent, n *Two in the Dark* Gelett Burgess, ph Jack MacKenzie, c Tom Conway. Amnesiac tries to prove himself innocent of murder.

*Two of a Kind* (1951) d Henry Levin, sc Lawrence Kimble, Gordon Kahn, n *Lefty Farrell* James Edward Grant, ph Burnett Guffey, c Edmond O'Brien, Lizabeth Scott. Long-lost son of rich parents turns out to be conman.

*Two Smart People* (1946) d Jules Dassin, sc Ethel Hill, Leslie Charteris, st Ralph Wheelright, Allan Kenward, ph Karl Freund, c Lucille Ball, John Hodiak. Two swindlers fall for each other whilst one is going to jail.

*Under the Gun* (1950) d Ted Tetzlaff, sc George Zuckerman, st Daniel B Ullman, ph Henry Freulich, c Richard Conte, Audrey Totter. In prison farm, gangster fights way to top.

*The Undercover Man* (1949) d Joseph H Lewis, sc Sydney Boehm, ar Frank J Wilson, st Jack Rubin, ph Burnett Guffey, c Glenn Ford. Docu Noir. Government agent goes undercover to get evidence on mobster.

*Undercurrent* (1946) d Vincente Minnelli, sc Edward Chodorov, n *You Were There* Thelma Strabel, ph Karl Freund, c Katharine Hepburn, Robert Taylor, Robert Mitchum. Woman gets between two brothers.

*Undertow* (1949) d William Castle, sc Arthur T Horman, Lee Loeb, st Horman, ph Irving Glassberg, c Scott Brady. War vet, framed for murder, races against time to prove innocence.

*The Underworld Story* (1950, *The Whipped*) d Cy Endfield, sc Henry Blankfort, ad Endfield, n *The Big Story* Craig Rice, ph Stanley Cortez, c Dan Duryea, Herbert Marshall. Reporter is involved with newspaper publisher.

*The Unfaithful* (1947) d Vincent Sherman, sc st David Goodis, ph Ernest Haller, c Ann Sheridan, Lew Ayres, Zachary Scott. Woman lies about intruder's death.

*Union Station* (1950) d Rudolp Maté, sc Sydney Boehm, st Thomas Walsh, ph Daniel L Fapp, c William Holden. Madman holds a blind girl hostage in Union Station.

*The Unknown Man* (1951) d Richard Thorpe, sc Ronald Miller, George Froeschel, ph William Mellor, c Walter Pidgeon. Lawyer crushed when he discovers man he successfully defended is guilty of murder.

*Unmasked* (1950) d George Blair, sc Albert DeMond, Norman S Hall, st Manuel Seff, Paul Yawitz, ph Ellis W Carter, c Robert Rockwell. Editor of sleazy newspaper gets money out of married woman, kills her and then frames the husband.

*The Unseen* (1945) d Lewis Allen, sc Hagar Wilde, Raymond Chandler, ad Wilde, Ken Englund, n *Her Heart in Her Throat* Ethel Lina White, ph John F Seitz, c Joel McCrea, Gail Russell, Herbert Marshall. Woman joins household whose master may be a killer.

*The Unsuspected* (1947) d Michael Curtiz, sc Ranald MacDougall, ad Bess Meredyth, n Charlotte Armstrong, ph Woody Bredell, c Claude Rains, Audrey Totter. Radio star plans and executes murder.

*Valerie* (1957) d Gerd Oswald, sc Leonard Heideman, Emmett Murphy, ph Ernest Laszlo, c Sterling Hayden, Anita Ekberg. Daughter vows to avenge parents' murder.

*The Velvet Touch* (1948) d John Gage, sc Leo Rosten, ad Walter N Reilly, st William Mercer, Annabel Ross, ph Joseph Walker, c Rosalind Russell, Claire Trevor, Sydney Greenstreet. Famous actress accidentally kills her producer and tries to cover it up.

*The Verdict* (1946) d Don Seigel, sc Peter Milne, n *The Big Bow Mystery* Israel Zangwill, ph Ernest Haller, c Sydney Greenstreet, Peter Lorre. Victorian ex-Scotland Yard detective tries to prove friend innocent of killing. 4/5

*Vertigo* (1958) d Alfred Hitchcock, sc Samuel A Taylor, Alec

Coppel, n *The Living and the Dead* Pierre Boileau, Thomas Narcejac, ph Robert Burks, c James Stewart, Kim Novak, Barbara Bel Geddes. Man becomes obsessed with woman, who commits suicide, then falls for girl who is her double. 5/5

*Vicki* (1953) d Harry Horner, sc Dwight Taylor, n *I Wake Up Screaming* Steve Fisher, ph Milton Krasner, c Jeanne Crain, Jean Peters. Detective becomes obsessed with death of girl.

*Violated* (1953) d Walter Strate, sc William Paul Miskin, c Wim Holland, Lili Dawn. Serial/sex killer haunts Greenwich Village killing and scalping women.

*Violence* (1947) d Jack Bernhard, sc Lewis Lantz, Stanley Rubin, ph Henry Sharp, c Nancy Coleman. Magazine writer goes uncovers a front for racketeers.

*Voice in the Wind* (1944) d Arthur Ripley, sc Frederick Torberg, st Ripley, ph Dick Fryer, c Francis Lederer. Pianist, victim of Nazis, lives on island of Guadalupe feeling depressed.

*Walk a Crooked Mile* (1948) d Gordon Douglas, sc George Bruce, st Bertram Millhauser, ph George Robinson, c Louis Hayward, Dennis O'Keefe. Secret Service break up mob with the help of Scotland Yard.

*Walk East on Beacon!* (1952, *The Crime of the Century*) d Alfred L Werker, sc Leonard Heideman, Emmett Murphy, Leo Rosten, Virginia Shaler, ar *The Crime of the Century* J Edgar Hoover, ph Joseph C Brun, c George Murphy. Docu Noir set in Boston.

*Walk Softly, Stranger* (1950) d Robert Stevenson, sc Frank Fenton, st Manny Seff, Paul Yawitz, ph Harry Wild, c Joseph Cotten, Valli. Thief hides out in small town and meets bitter girl confined to wheelchair.

*The Walls Came Tumbling Down* (1946) d Lothar Mendes, Wilfrid H Petitt, n Jo Eisinger, ph Charles Lawton Jr, c Lee Bowman. PI investigates priest's murder.

*The Web* (1947) d Michael Gordon, sc William Bowers, Bernard Millhauser, st Harry Kurnitz, ph Irving Glassberg, c Edmond O'Brien, Ella Raines. Lawyer protecting an industrialist is framed for murder.

*The Well* (1951) d Russell Rouse, sc Rouse, Clarence Greene, ph Ernest Laszlo, c Richard Rober. Black kid is trapped down well, igniting racial divisions.

*When Strangers Marry* (1944, *Betrayed*) d William Castle, sc Philip Yordan, Dennis J Cooper, st George V Mascov, ph Ira Morgan, c Dean Jagger, Kim Hunter, Robert Mitchum. Woman fears new husband is guilty of murder.

*Where Danger Lives* (1950) d John Farrow, sc Charles Bennett, st Leo Rosten, ph Nicholas Musuraca, c Robert Mitchum, Faith Domergue, Claude Rains. Doctor runs away with psychotic femme fatale after her husband is murdered.

*Where the Sidewalk Ends* (1950) d Otto Preminger, sc Ben Hecht, ad Victor Trivas, Frank P Rosenberg, Robert E Kent, n *Night Cry* William L Stuart, ph Joseph La Shelle, c Dana Andrews, Gene Tierney. Policeman kills suspect then frames gangster for crime.

*While the City Sleeps* (1956) d Fritz Lang, sc Cosey Robinson, n *The Bloody Spur* Charles Einstein, ph Ernest Laszlo, c Dana Andrews, Ida Lupino. Newspaper publisher offers editor's job to staff member who catches sex murderer – horrible society contrasted with relatively sympathetic killer. 4/5

*Whiplash* (1948) d Lewis Seiler, sc Maurice Geraghty, ad Gordon Kahn, st Kenneth Earl, ph Peverall Marley, c Dane Clark. Artist has an affair with woman whose husband convinces him to become fighter.

*Whirlpool* (1949) d Otto Preminger, sc Lester Bartow (aka Ben Hecht), Andrew Solt, n *Me Thinks the Lady* Guy Endore, ph Arthur Miller, c Gene Tierney, Richard Conte, Jose Ferrer. Mentally unbalanced woman used by hypnotist in murder plot.

*Whispering City* (1947) d Fedor Ozep, sc Rian James, Leonard Lee, st George Zuckerman, Michael Lennox, ph Guy Roe, c Helmut Dantine. Secrets of attorney's past uncovered by female reporter.

*Whispering Footsteps* (1943) d Howard Bretherton, sc Gertrude Walker, Dane Lussier, ph Jack Marta, c John Hubbard. Nightmare Noir. Bank clerk is spitting image of psychokiller.

*The Whistler* (1944) d William Castle, sc Eric Taylor, st J Donald Wilson, ph James S Brown Jr, c Richard Dix. Suicidal man hires hit man to kill him, then changes his mind but the hit man can't be stopped.

*Whistle Stop* (1946) d Leonide Moguy, sc Philip Yordan, st Maritta M Wolff, ph Russell Metty, c George Raft, Ava Gardner. Gambler thinks about murder when girlfriend dumps him.

*White Heat* (1949) d Raoul Walsh, sc Ivan Goff, Ben Roberts, st Virginia Kellogg, ph Sid Hickox, c James Cagney, Edmond O'Brien, Virginia Mayo. Psychotic gangster with mother fixation wages war against police.

*Why Must I Die?* (1960) d Roy Del Ruth, sc Richard Bernstein, George Waters, ph Ernest Haller, c Bert Freed, Terry Moore. Woman falsely accused of murder is put in the electric chair.

*Wicked Woman* (1954) d Russell Rouse, sc Clarence Greene, Rouse, ph Edward Fitzgerald, c Beverly Michaels, Richard Egan. Bar owner persuaded by femme fatale to rob wife and run for the border.

*The Window* (1949) d Ted Tetzlaff, sc Mel Dinelli, st *The Boy Who Cried Murder* Cornell Woolrich, ph William Steiner, c Barbara Hale, Bobby Driscoll. No one will believe boy who sees murder.

*Without Honor* (1950) d Irving Pichel, sc James Poe, ph Lionel Lindon, c Laraine Day. Woman thinks she has killed her lover.

*Without Warning* (1952) d Arnold Laven, sc Bill Raynor, ph Joseph Biroc, c Adam Williams. Docu Noir. Police search for killer of blondes.

*Witness to Murder* (1954) d Roy Rowland, sc Chester Erskine, ph John Alton, c Barbara Stanwyck, George Sanders. No one will believe businesswoman who sees murder.

*Woman in Hiding* (1940) d Michael Gordon, sc Oscar Saul, ph William Daniels, c Ida Lupino, Howard Duff, Stephen McNally. Woman runs away from violent husband and meets man who wants to take her back.

*The Woman in the Window* (1944) d Fritz Lang, sc Nunnally Johnson, n *Once Off Guard* J H Wallis, ph Milton Krasner, c Edward G Robinson, Joan Bennett, Dan Duryea. Professor flirts with woman and enters nightmare. 4/5

*The Woman in White* (1948) d Peter Godfrey, sc Stephen Morehouse Avery, n Wilkie Collins, ph Carl Guthrie, c Eleanor Parker, Alexis Smith, Sydney Greenstreet. Gothic Noir. Woman's double gives warning against Count.

*The Woman on Pier 13* (1949, *I Married a Communist!*) d Robert Stevenson, sc Charles Grayson, Robert Hardy Andrews, st George W George, George Slavin, ph Nicholas Musuraca, c Laraine Day, Robert Ryan. Rouge Noir. Shipping executive told by Communists to take over labour union.

*The Woman on the Beach* (1947) d Jean Renoir, sc Renoir, Frank Davis, n *None So Blind* Mitchell Wilson, ph Leo Tover, c Joan Bennett, Robert Ryan. War vet gets involved with wife of blind painter.

*Woman on the Run* (1950) d Norman Foster, sc Alan Campbell, Foster, st Sylvia Tate, ph Hal Mohr, c Ann Sheridan, Dennis O'Keefe. Woman helps police find husband who is in hiding because he saw murder.

*A Woman's Face* (1941) d George Cukor, sc Donald Ogden Stewart, pl Francis de Croisset, ph Robert Plack, c Joan

Crawford. Hideously scarred woman runs a blackmailing ring.

*A Woman's Secret* (1949) d Nicholas Ray, sc Herman J Mankiewicz, n *Mortgage on Life* Vicki Baum, ph George E Diskant, c Maureen O'Hara, Melvyn Douglas, Gloria Grahame. Flashbacks explain why one woman shot another.

*Women's Prison* (1955) d Lewis Seiler, sc Crane Wilbur, Jack DeWitt, ph Lester H White, c Ida Lupino. Life of inmates is hell thanks to head guard.

*A Woman's Vengeance* (1948, *The Giaconda Smile*) d Zoltan Korda, sc Aldous Huxley, ph Russell Metty, c Charles Boyer, Jessica Tandy, Ann Blyth. Country house noir.

*World for Ransom* (1954) d Robert Aldrich, sc Lindsay Hardy, ph Joseph Biroc, c Dan Duryea, Gene Lockhart. Private eye tries to prevent the kidnapping of nuclear scientist.

*The Wrong Man* (1956) d Alfred Hitchcock, sc Maxwell Anderson, Angus MacPhail, st Anderson, ph Robert Burks, c Henry Fonda, Vera Miles. Docu Noir. Musician's life is ruined because he resembles hold-up man. 5/5

## Noir Westerns

*The Return of Frank James* (1940) d Fritz Lang
*Pursued* (1947) d Raoul Walsh
*Ramrod* (1947) d André de Toth
*Station West* (1948) d Sidney Lanfield
*The Furies* (1950) d Anthony Mann
*Winchester '73* (1950) d Anthony Mann
*The Naked Spur* (1953) d Anthony Mann

## Post-Noir (1961–1975)

*Blast of Silence* (1961) d Allen Baron
*Man-Trap* (1961) d Edmond O'Brien

*Underworld USA* (1961) d Sam Fuller
*Cape Fear* (1962) d J Lee Thompson
*Experiment in Terror* (1962) d Blake Edwards
*The Manchurian Candidate* (1962) d John Frankenheimer
*War Hunt* (1962) d Denis Sanders
*The Killers* (1964) d Don Seigel
*The Naked Kiss* (1964) d Sam Fuller
*Angel's Flight* (1965)
*Brainstorm* (1965) d William Conrad
*Who Killed Teddy Bear* (1965) d Joseph Cates
*Harper* (1966) d Jack Smight
*The Money Trap* (1965) d Burt Kennedy
*Point Blank* (1967) d John Boorman
*Warning Shot* (1967) d Buzz Kulik
*The Detective* (1968) d Gordon Douglas
*Lady in Cement* (1968) d Gordon Douglas
*Madigan* (1968) d Don Seigel
*Night of the Following Day* (1968) d Hubert Cornfield
*The Split* (1968) d Gordon Flemyng
*Marlowe* (1969) d Paul Bogart
*The Kremlin Letter* (1970) d John Huston
*Venus in Furs* (1970) d Jesús Franco
*Dirty Harry* (1971) d Don Seigel
*The French Connection* (1971) d William Friedkin
*Klute* (1971) d Alan Pakula
*Chandler* (1972) d Paul Magwood
*Hickey & Boggs* (1972) d Robert Culp
*The Friends of Eddie Coyle* (1973) d Peter Yates
*The Long Goodbye* (1973) d Robert Altman
*Serpico* (1973) d Sidney Lumet
*Black Eye* (1974) d Jack Arnold
*Bring Me the Head of Alfredo Garcia* (1974) d Sam Peckinpah
*Chinatown* (1974) d Roman Polanski
*The Conversation* (1974) d Francis Ford Coppola

*Death Wish* (1974) d Michael Winner
*The Outfit* (1974) d John Flynn
*The Parallax View* (1974) d Alan Pakula
*Thieves Like Us* (1974) d Robert Altman
*Dog Day Afternoon* (1975) d Sidney Lumet
*The Drowning Pool* (1975) d Stuart Rosenberg
*Farewell, My Lovely* (1975) d Dick Richards
*French Connection II* (1975) d John Frankenheimer
*Hustle* (1975) d Robert Aldrich
*Night Moves* (1975) d Arthur Penn
*The Nickel Ride* (1975) d Robert Mulligan
*Three Days of the Condor* (1975) d Sydney Pollack

## Neo-Noir (1976–1992)

*The Killer Inside Me* (1976) d Burt Kennedy
*The Killing of a Chinese Bookie* (1976) d John Cassavetes
*Special Delivery* (1976) d Paul Wendkos
*Taxi Driver* (1976) d Martin Scorsese
*American Friend* (1977) d Wim Wenders
*Rolling Thunder* (1977) d John Flynn
*The Big Sleep* (1978) d Michael Winner
*The Driver* (1978) d Walter Hill
*Who'll Stop the Rain* (1978) d Karel Reisz
*Hardcore* (1979) d Paul Schrader
*Last Embrace* (1979) d Jonathan Demme
*The Onion Field* (1979) d Harold Becker
*The First Deadly Sin* (1980) d Brian G Hutton
*Union City* (1980) d Mark Reichert
*Atlantic City* (1981) d Louis Malle
*Body Heat* (1981) d Lawrence Kasdan
*Eyewitness* (1981, *The Janitor*) d Peter Yates
*Ms 45* (1981) d Abel Ferrara
*The Postman Always Rings Twice* (1981) d Bob Rafelson

*Prince of the City* (1981) d Sidney Lumet

*Sharky's Machine* (1981) d Burt Reynolds

*Thief* (1981, *Violent Streets* in UK) d Michael Mann

*True Confessions* (1981) d Ulu Grosbard

*Blade Runner* (1982) d Ridley Scott

*The Border* (1982) d Tony Richardson

*Dead Men Don't Wear Plaid* (1982) d Carl Reiner

*48 Hours* (1982) d Walter Hill

*I, the Jury* (1982) d Richard T Heffron

*Still of the Night* (1982) d Robert Benton

*Bad Boys* (1983) d Richard Rosenthal

*Breathless* (1983) d James Bridges

*Hammett* (1983) d Wim Wenders

*Sudden Impact* (1983) d Clint Eastwood

*Against All Odds* (1984) d Taylor Hackford

*Blood Simple* (1984) d Joel Coen

*Fear City* (1984) d Abel Ferrara

*Mike's Murder* (1984) d James Bridges

*Tightrope* (1984) d Richard Tuggle

*Jagged Edge* (1985) d Richard Marquand

*To Live and Die in LA* (1985) d William Friedkin

*Witness* (1985) d Peter Weir

*Year of the Dragon* (1985) d Michael Cimino

*At Close Range* (1986) d James Foley

*Blue Velvet* (1986) d David Lynch

*Dangerously Close* (1986) d Albert Pyun

*Eight Million Ways to Die* (1986) d Hal Ashby

*52-Pick-Up* (1986) d John Frankenheimer

*Manhunter* (1986) d Michael Mann

*The Morning After* (1986) d Sidney Lumet

*Murphy's Law* (1986) d J Lee Thompson

*No Mercy* (1986) d Richard Pearce

*Out of Bounds* (1986) d Richard Tuggle

*Angel Heart* (1987) d Alan Parker

*The Bedroom Window* (1987) d Curtis Hanson
*Best Seller* (1987) d John Flynn
*The Big Easy* (1987) d Jim McBride
*Black Widow* (1987) d Bob Rafelson
*Fatal Attraction* (1987) d Adrian Lyne
*House of Games* (1987) d David Mamet
*The Killing Time* (1987) d Rick King
*Lady Beware* (1987) d Karen Arthur
*Lethal Weapon* (1987) d Richard Donner
*Malone* (1987) d Harley Cokliss
*No Way Out* (1987) d Roger Donaldson
*PI Private Investigations* (1987) d Nigel Dick
*Positive ID* (1987) d Andy Anderson
*Rosary Murders* (1987) d Fred Walton
*Slamdance* (1987) d Wayne Wang
*Someone to Watch Over Me* (1987) d Ridley Scott
*Stripped to Kill* (1987) d Katt Shea Ruben
*Suspect* (1987) d Peter Yates
*Betrayed* (1988) d Constantin Costa-Gavras
*Call Me* (1988) d Sollace Mitchell
*Cop* (1988) d James B Harris
*DOA* (1988) d Rocky Morton, Annabel Jankel
*Frantic* (1988) d Roman Polanski
*Masquerade* (1988) d Bob Swaim
*Shoot to Kill* (1988) d Roger Spottiswoode
*Tequila Sunrise* (1988) d Robert Towne
*White of the Eye* (1988) d Donald Cammell
*Black Rain* (1989) d Ridley Scott
*Cat Chaser* (1989) d Abel Ferrara
*Criminal Law* (1989) d Martin Campbell
*Dead-Bang* (1989) d John Frankenheimer
*Drugstore Cowboy* (1989) d Gus Van Sant
*Gleaming the Cube* (1989) d Graeme Clifford
*Hit List* (1989) d William Lustig

*Johnny Handsome* (1989) d Walter Hill
*Lethal Weapon II* (1989) d Richard Donner
*Night Visitor* (1989) d Rupert Hitzig
*Out of the Dark* (1989) d Michael Schroeder
*Paint it Black* (1989) d Tim Hunter
*Prime Suspect* (1989) d Mark Rutland
*Relentless* (1989) d William Lustig
*Sea of Love* (1989) d Harold Becker
*True Believer* (1989) d Joseph Ruben
*After Dark, My Sweet* (1990) d James Foley
*Alligator Eyes* (1990) d John Feldman
*Another 48 Hours* (1990) d Walter Hill
*Bad Influence* (1990) d Curtis Hanson
*Blue Steel* (1990) d Kathryn Bigelow
*Body Chemistry* (1990) d Kristine Peterson
*Desperate Hours* (1990) d Michael Cimino
*Genuine Risk* (1990) d Kurt Voss
*The Grifters* (1990) d Stephen Frears
*The Hot Spot* (1990) d Dennis Hopper
*Impulse* (1990) d Sondra Locke
*Internal Affairs* (1990) d Michael Figgis
*Jezebel's Kiss* (1990) d Harvey Keith
*Kill Me Again* (1990) d John Dahl
*The Kill-Off* (1990) d Maggie Greenwald
*King of New York* (1990) d Abel Ferrara
*Miami Blues* (1990) d George Armitage
*Miller's Crossing* (1990) d Joel Coen
*Mortal Passions* (1990) d Andrew Lane
*Narrow Margin* (1990) d Peter Hyams
*New Jack City* (1990) d Mario Van Peebles
*Out of the Rain* (1990) d Gary Winick
*Pacific Heights* (1990) d John Schlesinger
*Presumed Innocent* (1990) d Alan Pakula
*Q&A* (1990) d Sidney Lumet

*The Rain Killer* (1990) d Ken Stein
*Revenge* (1990) d Kevin Reynolds
*Sleeping With the Enemy* (1990) d Joseph Ruben
*State of Grace* (1990) d Phil Joanou
*The Two Jakes* (1990) d Jack Nicholson
*Cape Fear* (1991) d Martin Scorsese
*Dead Again* (1991) d Kenneth Branagh
*Deceived* (1991) d Michael Finnell
*Delusion* (1991) d Carl Colpaert
*Femme Fatale* (1991) d Andre Guttfreund
*Homicide* (1991) d David Mamet
*The Horseplayer* (1991) d Kurt Voss
*Intimate Stranger* (1991) d Allan Holzman
*A Kiss Before Dying* (1991) d James Dearden
*Kiss Me a Killer* (1991) d Marcus DeLeon
*The Last Boy Scout* (1991) d Tony Scott
*Liebestraum* (1991) d Michael Figgis
*Mortal Thoughts* (1991) d Alan Rudolph
*Point Break* (1991) d Kathryn Bigelow
*Run* (1991) d Geoff Burrowes
*Rush* (1991) d Lili Fini Zanuck
*Scissors* (1991) d Frank De Felitta
*Shattered* (1991) d Wolfgang Petersen
*Silence of the Lambs* (1991) d Jonathan Demme
*Thelma and Louise* (1991) d Ridley Scott
*VI Warshawski* (1991) d Jeff Kanew
*Basic Instinct* (1992) d Paul Verhoeven
*Blue Desert* (1992) d Bradford Battersby
*The Bodyguard* (1992) d Mick Jackson
*Criminal Intent* (1992) d Woth Ketter
*The Dark Wind* (1992) d Errol Morris
*Deep Cover* (1992) d Bill Duke
*Diary of a Hitman* (1992) d Roy London
*Final Analysis* (1992) d Phil Joanou

*Guncrazy* (1992) d Tamra Davis
*The Hand That Rocks the Cradle* (1992) d Curtis Hanson
*Lethal Weapon III* (1992) d Richard Donner
*Love Crimes* (1992) d Lizzie Borden
*Midnight Heat* (1992) d John Nicolella
*Nails* (1992) d John Flynn
*Night and the City* (1992) d Irwin Winkler
*Past Midnight* (1992) d Jan Eliaberg
*Red Rock West* (1992) d John Dahl
*Reservoir Dogs* (1992) d Quentin Tarantino
*Thunderheart* (1992) d Michael Apted
*To Kill For* (1992) d John Dirlam
*White Sands* (1992) d Roger Donaldson

## France

*Portrait D'Un Assassin* (1949) d Bernard-Roland
*Casque D'Or* (1952) d Jacques Becker
*Rififi* (1954) d Jules Dassin
*Touchez Pas au Grisbi* (1954) d Jacques Becker
*Les Diaboliques* (1955) d Henri-Georges Clouzot
*Section des Disparus* (1956) d Pierre Chenal
*Ascenseur Pour L'Echafaud* (1958, *Lift to the Scaffold*) d Louis
    Malle
*Plein Soleil* (1958, *Purple Noon*) d Jean Renoir
*A Bout de Souffle* (1959) d Jean-Luc Godard
*Two Men in Manhattan* (1959) d Jean-Pierre Melville
*Tirez Sur le Pianiste* (1960, *Shoot the Piano Player*) d François
    Truffaut
*Le Doulos* (1962) d Jean-Pierre Melville
*Alphaville* (1965) d Jean-Luc Godard
*Pierrot le Fou* (1965) d Jean-Luc Godard
*Second Breath* (1967) d Jean-Pierre Melville
*Le Samouräi* (1967) d Jean-Pierre Melville

*La Mariée Etait en Noir* (1968, *The Bride Wore Black*) d François Truffaut

*La Sirène du Mississippi* (1969, *Mississippi Mermaid*) d François Truffaut

*This Man Must Die* (1969) d Claude Chabrol

*The Butcher* (1970) d Claude Chabrol

*Le Cercle Rouge* (1970) d Jean-Pierre Melville

*Le Casse* (1971) d Henri Verneuil

*La Course du Lièvre a Travers les Champs* (1972) d RenéClément

*The Outside Man* (1973) d Jacques Deray

*Série Noire* (1979) d Alain Corneau

*Clean Slate* (1981, *Coup De Torchon*) d Bertrand Tavernier

*La Lune Dans le Caniveau* (1983) d Jean-Jacques Beineix

*Street of the Damned* (1984, Rue Barbare) d Giles Behat

*Descente aux Enfers* (1986) d Francis Girod

*Street of No Return* (1989, *Sans Espoir de Retour*) d Sam Fuller

*La Femme Nikita* (1991) d Luc Besson

## UK

*The Lodger* (1927) d Alfred Hitchcock

*Blackmail* (1929) d Alfred Hitchcock

*They Drive by Night* (1938) d Arthur B Woods

*I Met a Murderer* (1939) d Roy Kellino

*On the Night of the Fire* (1939) d Brian Desmond Hurst

*There Ain't No Justice* (1939) d Pen Tennyson

*The Man in Grey* (1943) d Leslie Arliss

*Appointment With Crime* (1945) d John Harlow

*Dead of Night* (1945) d Alberto Cavalcanti, Charles Crichton, Basil Dearden, Robert Hamer

*Wanted for Murder* (1946, *A Voice in the Night*) d Lawrence Huntington

*Brighton Rock* (1947) d John Boulting

*Dancing With Crime* (1947) d John Paddy Carstairs

*Daybreak* (1947) d Compton Bennett

*Dear Murderer* (1947) d Arthur Crabtree

*Frieda* (1947) d Basil Dearden

*Mine Own Executioner* (1947) d Anthony Kimmins

*The October Man* (1947) d Roy Ward Baker

*Odd Man Out* (1947) d Carol Reed

*They Made Me a Fugitive* (1947) d Alberto Cavalcanti

*The Upturned Glass* (1947) d Lawrence Huntington

*The Fallen Idol* (1948) d Carol Reed

*It Always Rains on Sunday* (1948) d Robert Hamer

*Night Beat* (1948) d Harold Huth

*Noose* (1948) d Edmund T Gréville

*For Them That Trespass* (1949) d Alberto Cavalcanti

*Give Us This Day* (1949) d Edward Dmytryk

*Good Time Girl* (1949) d David MacDonald

*The Third Man* (1949) d Carol Reed

*Guilty Is My Shadow* (1950) d Roy Kellino

*Seven Days to Noon* (1950) d Roy and John Boulting

*Cloudburst* (1951) d Francis Searle

*The Clouded Yellow* (1951) d Ralph Thomas

*The Gambler and the Lady* (1952) d Patrick Jenkins, Sam Newfield

*A Stolen Face* (1952) d Terence Fisher

*The Fake* (1953) d Godfrey Grayson

*The Flanagan Boy* (1953, *Bad Blonde, The Woman is Trouble*) d Reginald Le Borg

*36 Hours* (1953) d Montgomery Tully

*Time Bomb* (1953, *Terror On A Train*) d Ted Tetzlaff

*Five Days* (1954, *Paid to Kill*) d Montgomery Tully

*The Good Die Young* (1954) d Lewis Gilbert

*Murder by Proxy* (1954, *Blackout*) d Terence Fisher

*Confession* (1956, *The Deadliest Sin*) d Ken Hughes

*Intimate Stranger* (1956, *Finger of Guilt*) d Joseph Losey

*Tiger in the Smoke* (1956) d Roy Ward Baker

*Yeild to the Night* (1956, *Blonde Sinner*) d J Lee Thompson
*Cast a Dark Shadow* (1957) d Lewis Gilbert
*Chase a Crooked Shadow* (1957) d Michael Anderson
*Footsteps in the Fog* (1957) d Arthur Lubin
*Hidden Homicde* (1958) d Anthony Young
*The Man Who Wouldn't Talk* (1958) d Herbert Wilcox
*Nowhere to Go* (1958) d Seth Holt, Basil Dearden
*Violent Playground* (1958) d Basil Dearden
*The End of the Line* (1959) d Charles Saunders
*Peeping Tom* (1959) d Michael Powell
*Subway in the Sky* (1959) d Muriel Box
*The Criminal* (1960) d Joseph Losey
*Hell Is a City* (1960) d Val Guest
*Payroll* (1961) d Sidney Hayers
*Jigsaw* (1962) d Val Guest
*Hell Drivers* (1967) d Cy Endfield
*Robbery* (1967) d Peter Yates
*Performance* (1969) d Nicholas Roeg, Donald Cammell
*Revenge* (1971) d Sidney Hayers
*Get Carter* (1971) d Mike Hodges
*Pulp* (1972) d Mike Hodges
*The Long Good Friday* (1982) d John Mackenzie
*The Hit* (1984) d Stephen Frears
*Defense of the Realm* (1985) d David Drury
*The McGuffin* (1985) d Colin Bucksey
*Stormy Monday* (1988) d Mike Figgis
*The Krays* (1991) d Peter Medak

## Italy

*Ossessione* (1943) d Luchino Visconti
*La Strada Buia* (1949, *Fugitive Lady*) d Sidney Salkow, Marino
    Girolami
*Blood and Black Lace* (1964) d Mario Bava

*The Bird With the Crystal Plumage* (1969) d Dario Argento
*The Conformist* (1971) d Bernardo Bertolucci

## Mexico

*Dinero Maldito* (1949, *La Ciudad*) d Fernando A Rivero
*Tinieblas* (1957) d José Diaz Morales
*Secuestro en Acapulco* (1960) d Federico Curiel

## Japan

*High and Low* (1962) d Akira Kurosawa, n Ed McBain
*Branded to Kill* (1967) d Seijun Suzuki
*Violated Women in White* (1967) d Koji Wakamatsu
*Battles Without Honour and Humility* (1973) d Kinji Fukasaku
*Graveyard of Honour and Humanity* (1975) d Kinji Fukasaku
*Violent Cop* (1989) d Takashi Kitano
*Boiling Point* (1990) d Takashi Kitano
*Sonatine* (1993) d Takashi Kitano
*Hana-Bi* (1997) d Takashi Kitano
*Brother* (2000) d Takashi Kitano

# Resource Materials

## Books About Film Noir

*America Noir: Underground Writers and Filmmakers of the Postwar Era* by David Cochran, Smithsonian Institute Press.

*The American Roman Noir* by William Marling, University Of Georgia Press.

*The Art of Noir* by Eddie Muller, Overlook, 2002. A fabulous full-colour guide to Film Noir posters.

*The Big Book of Noir* ed Ed Gorman, Lee Server & Martin H Greenberg, Carroll & Graf, 1998. A great big book featuring Lang, Wilder, Siodmak, Karlson, Mainwaring, *Naked City*, *Night and the City*, and others from the Film Noir world. It also has a large section on Noir Fiction, including Woolrich, Thompson, Gil Brewer, Harry Whittington, Peter Rabe and others. A valuable reference.

*Crime Scenes: Movie Poster Art of the Film Noir: The Classic Period: 1941–1959* by Lawrence Bassoff, Lawrence Bassoff Collection Inc.

*Dark Cinema* by Jon Tuska, Greenwood, 1984.

*Dark City: The Film Noir* by Spencer Selby, St James Press, 1984. Excellent reference with analysis of 25 Film Noirs, then comprehenisive appendices.

*Dark City: The Lost World of Film Noir* by Eddie Muller, St Martin's Press, 1998. Entertaining summation of Film Noirs, giving a history of Hollywood's dark past as well as the stories behind the movies. Profusely illustrated and featuring a colour poster gallery.

*Dark City Dames* by Eddie Muller, Regan Books, 2001. Six femme fatales are interviewed.

*The Dark Side of the Screen: Film Noir* by Foster Hirsch, A S Barnes, 1981.

*Detours and Lost Highways: A Map of Neo-Noir* by Foster Hirsch, Proscenium/Limelight.

*The Devil Thumbs a Ride & Other Unforgettable Films* by Barry Gifford, Grove Press, 1988. Idiosyncratic selection of movies with personal comments from Noir Fictioneer Gifford.

*Film Noir: A Comprehensive, Illustrated Reference to Movies* by Michael L Stephens, McFarland & Co, 1994.

*Film Noir: An Encyclopaedic Reference to the American Style* ed Alain Silver & Elizabeth Ward, Third Edition, The Overlook Press, 1992. An enormous book featuring detailed synopses and analysis of 300 Film Noirs, plus articles & appendices, which makes it an essential book in your Film Noir library.

*Film Noir Reader* ed Alain Silver & James Ursini, Limelight Editions, 1996. A collection of seminal essays from the past (see Articles section below), case studies of specific films, and general articles around a subject.

*Film Noir Reader 2* ed Alain Silver & James Ursini, Limelight Editions, 1999. More of the same.

*Film Noir Reader 3* ed Robert Porfirio, Alain Silver & James Ursini, Limelight Editions, 2002. Interviews with eight directors and ten other filmmakers of the classic noir period.

*Film Noir: Reflections in a Dark Mirror* by Bruce Crowther, Columbus Books, 1988. A by-the-numbers look at Film Noir writers, directors, actors and themes. Lots of large photos.

*Hard-Boiled: Great Lines From Classic Noir Films* by Peggy Thompson & Saeko Usukawa, Studio Vista, 1995. An excellent book full of quotes from lots of Film Noirs. Not only that, but there are some nice photos as well.

*Hollywood in the Forties* by Charles Higham & Joel Greenberg, A S Barnes, 1968. One chapter is the first survey of Film Noir in the English language.

*Hollywood's Dark Cinema: The American Film Noir* by R Barton Palmer, Twayne.

*Mean Streets and Raging Bulls: The Legacy of Film Noir in Contemporary American Cinema* by Richard Martin, Scarecrow Press, 1999.

*More Than Night: Film Noir in its Contexts* by James Naremore, University of California Press.

*The Movie Book of Film Noir* ed Ian Cameron, Studio Vista, 1992. As well as analysis on individual Film Noirs, there are articles on the French Poetic Realist movies of the 1930s, a big section on Robert Siodmak, and a couple of articles on Neo-Noirs.

*Panorama du Film Noir Américain* by Raymond Borde & Etienne Chaumeton, 1955.

*Perspectives on Film Noir* ed R Barton Palmer, G K Hall.

*A Reference Guide to the American Film Noir: 1940–1958* by Robert Ottoson, Scarecrow Press, 1981.

*Shades of Noir* ed Joan Copjec, Verso, 1993. An eclectic collection of articles which feature Cornell Woolrich, Chandler, the spaces in Film Noir, Noir by coloured people, etc. Most interesting is the assertion that *The Big Gamble* (1931) was the first Film Noir.

*Somewhere in the Night: Film Noir and the American City* by Nicholas Christopher, Owl Books, 1997.

*Towards a Definition of the American Film Noir* by Amir Massourd Karimi, Arno Press, 1970.

*Voices in the Dark: The Narrative Patterns of Film Noir* by J P Telotte, University of Illinois Press, 1989.

*Women in Film Noir* ed E Ann Kaplan, BFI, 1978. Influential and much-quoted book about... er women in Film Noir.

## Books About Film Noir Directors

*Alfred Hitchcock* by Paul Duncan, Pocket Essential, 1999, ISBN 1-903047-00-5, £3.99.

*The Director's Event* by Eric Sherman & Martin Rubin, Atheneum, 1970. Interviews with Budd Boetticher, Peter Bogdanovich, Samuel Fuller, Arthur Penn & Abraham Polonsky.

*Sam Fuller* by Nicholas Garnham, BFI, 1971.

*Sam Fuller: Film is a Battleground: A Critical Study* by Lee Server, McFarland & Co, 1994.

*Stanley Kubrick* by Paul Duncan, Pocket Essential, 1999, ISBN 1-903047-01-3, £3.99.

*Fritz Lang* by Lotte Eisner, Secker & Warbutg, 1976. Excellent analysis of films by one of Lang's friends.

*Fritz Lang: The Nature of the Beast* by Patrick McGillian, St Martin's Press, 1997. An extraordinary biography of Lang – the best – reveals a far more complex and manipulative man than we ever suspected before.

*Joseph Losey: A Revenge on Life* by David Caute, Faber & Faber, 1994.

*Queen of the B's: Ida Lupino Behind the Camera* ed Annette Kuhn, Praeger, 1995.

*Nicholas Ray: An American Journey* by Bernard Eisenschitz, Faber & Faber, 1993.

*Robert Siodmak: A Biography, With Critical Analyses of His Films Noirs and a Filmography of All His Works* by Deborah Lazaroff Alpi, McFarland, 1998.

*Orson Welles* by Martin Fitzgerald, Pocket Essential, 2000, ISBN 1-903047-04-8, £3.99.

*Who the Devil Made It* by Peter Bogdanovich, Ballantine, 1998. A great, great book featuring articles and interviews with Film Noir directors Aldrich, Dwan, Hawks, Hitchcock, Lang, Lewis, Lumet, Preminger, Siegel, von

Sternberg, Ulmer and Walsh. Beg, borrow or steal this book!

*Billy Wilder* by Glenn Hopp, Pocket Essential, 2001.

## Books About Film Noir Writers

*Backstory* ed Pat McGilligan, University Of California Press, 1986. Interviews with screenwriters including Charles Bennett, W R Burnett, Niven Busch, James M Cain, Lenore Coffee and others.

*Cain* by Roy Hoopes, Holt Rinehart Winston, 1982. A biography of James M Cain.

*Raymond Chandler and Film* by William Luhr, Ungar, 1982.

*Raymond Chandler in Hollywood* by Al Clark, Proteus, 1982.

*Difficult Lives* by James Sallis, Gryphon Publications, 1993. Three long articles on Jim Thompson, David Goodis and Chester Himes.

*Dashiell Hammett: A Life* by Diane Johnson, Random House, 1983. Probably the best-written biography.

*Dashiell Hammett: A Life on the Edge* by William F Nolan, Congdon & Weed, 1983. Probably the best-researched biography.

*Noir Fiction* by Paul Duncan, Pocket Essential, 2000, ISBN 1-903047-11-0 £3.99. Features sections on Horace McCoy, Jim Thompson, David Goodis, Cornell Woolrich and others whose books were adapted for Film Noir, or who wrote screenplays. Has an extensive list of other reference sources.

*Jim Thompson: Sleep With the Devil* by Michael J McCauley, Mysterious Press, 1991.

*Savage Art: A Biography of Jim Thompson* by Robert Polito, Serpent's Tail, 1997, ISBN 1-85242-571-7, £15.00. The best biography on Noir Fiction's golden boy.

*Tough Guy Writers of the Thirties* edited by David Madden, Southern Illinois University Press, 1968. Articles about

Noir and Hard-Boiled writers including Cain, Gresham, Thompson and McCoy.

*Nathanael West: The Art of His Life* by Jay Martin, Farrar, Strauss & Giroux, 1970.

*Cornell Woolrich: First You Dream, Then You Die* by Francis M Nevins, Mysterious Press, 1988.

## Articles

FNR = Reprinted in *Film Noir Reader*. FNR2 = Reprinted in *Film Noir Reader 2*.

*Americans Are Also Making Noir Films* by Jean-Pierre Chartier, *Revue du Cinéma 2*, 1946, FNR2.

*Crime Certainly Pays on the Screen* by Lloyd Shearer, 1945, FNR2.

*The Evolution of the Crime Drama* by Claude Chabrol, *Cahiers du Cinéma 54*, 1955, FNR2.

*The Filmic Transaction: On the Openings of Film Noirs* by Marc Vernet, *Velvet Light Trap 20*, Summer 1983, FNR2.

*Film Noir: A Modest Proposal* by James Damico, *Film Reader 3*, 1978, FNR.

*Film Noir: Society, Violence and the Bitch Goddess* by Stephen Farber, *Film Comment 10*, 1974, FNR2.

*Film Noir: Style and Content* by Dale E Ewing, Jr, *Journal of Popular Film and Television 16*, Summer 1988, FNR2.

*A New Kind of Police Drama: The Criminal Adventure* by Nino Frank, *L'Ecran Français 61*, 1946, FNR2.

*Noir Cinema* by Charles Higham & Joel Greenberg, *Hollywood in the Forties*, 1968, FNR.

*Notes of Film Noir* by Paul Schrader, *Film Comment*, Spring 1972, FNR.

*No Way Out: Existential Motifs in the Film Noir* by Robert G Porfirio, *Sight and Sound*, Autumn 1976, FNR.

*Out of What Past? Notes on the B Film Noir* by Paul Kerr,

*Screen*, 1979, FNR.

*Paint it Black: The Family Tree of Film Noir* by Raymond Durgnat, *Cinema* (UK), August 1970, FNR.

*Some Visual Motifs of Film Noir* by J A Place & L S Peterson, *Film Comment*, January 1974, FNR.

*Towards a Definition of Film Noir* by Raymond Borde & Etienne Chaumeton, *Panorama du Film Noir Américain*, 1955, FNR.

*Three Faces of Film Noir* by Tom Flinn, *Velvet Light Trap 5*, 1972, FNR2.

## Websites

*The 'Danger & Despair Knitting Circle' Video Club* – *www.noir-film.com* –This is a group of Film Noir fans who decided to have one place where they can store all their Film Noirs and it has turned into a worldwide hunt. They trade copies of their films for films they want. You can also buy copies. What's more, you can talk to other Film Noir fanatics, and find out about Film Noir festivals etc.

*Total Directory of Film* – http://www.tdfilm.com/genres/filmnoir.html – has links to Film Noir sites, including the ten Shades of Noir section of Images Journal, and Alain Silver's Film Noir Reader site. These sites have a wonderful mixture of text, analysis, quotes, sound bytes, film clips, film posters and photos.

# Index

These index entires have been obtained solely from the text preceding the Filmography. Although page numbers have been included for those entries that appear in both sections, there are no index entries for anything that is referred to in the Filmography alone.

# POCKET ESSENTIALS STOCK TITLES

| | |
|---|---|
| 1904048625 | Alchemy & Alchemists  Sean Martin  9.99 hb |
| 1903047722 | American Civil War  Phil Davies  3.99 |
| 1903047730 | American Indian Wars  Howard Hughes  3.99 |
| 1903047757 | Ancient Greece  Mike Paine  3.99 |
| 1903047854 | The Beat Generation  Jamie Russell  3.99 |
| 1903047919 | Bisexuality  Angie Bowie  3.99 |
| 1903047749 | Black Death  Sean Martin  3.99 |
| 1904048978 | Bruce Springsteen  4.99 |
| 1904048099 | Creative Writing  Neil Nixon  3.99 |
| 1904048382 | The Crusades  Mike Paine  9.99 hb |
| 1904048277 | Do Your Own PR  Richard Milton  3.99 |
| 190304751X | Feminism  Susan Osborne  3.99 |
| 1904048080 | Film Studies  Andrew M Butler  4.99 |
| 190304748X | Filming on a Microbudget NE Paul Hardy  4.99 |
| 1903047544 | Freud & Psychoanalysis  Nick Rennison  3.99 |
| 1904048218 | Georges Simenon  David Carter  3.99 |
| 1904048161 | Globalisation  Steven P McGiffen  3.99 |
| 1903047994 | History of Witchcraft  Lois Martin  3.99 |
| 1904048692 | Jack the Ripper  Whitehead/Rivett  9.99 hb |
| 1904048188 | Jethro Tull  Raymond Benson  3.99 |
| 1904048285 | The Knights Templar  Sean Martin  9.99 hb |
| 1903047609 | Laurel & Hardy  Brian J Robb  3.99 |
| 1903047803 | The Madchester Scene  Richard Luck  3.99 |
| 1903047498 | Nietzsche  Travis Elborough  3.99 |
| 1904048676 | Noir Fiction  Paul Duncan  4.99 |
| 1904048226 | Nuclear Paranoia  C Newkey-Burden  3.99 |
| 1903047293 | Philip K Dick  Andrew M Butler  3.99 |
| 1904048242 | Postmodernism  Andrew M Butler  3.99 |
| 1903047838 | The Rise of New Labour  Robin Ramsay  3.99 |
| 1903047684 | Sherlock Holmes  Mark Campbell  3.99 |
| 1903047331 | Stock Market Essentials  Victor Cuadra  3.99 |
| 1904048064 | Succeed in Music Business  Paul Charles  3.99 |
| 1903047390 | Terry Pratchett  Andrew M Butler  3.99 |
| 1903047889 | UFOs  Neil Nixon  3.99 |
| 190404882X | The Universe  Richard Osborne  9.99 hb |
| 1904048358 | Urban Legends  4.99 |
| 1904048129 | Who Shot JFK?  Robin Ramsay  3.99 |
| 1903047471 | Writing a Screenplay  John Costello  4.99 |

Or browse all our titles at www.pocketessentials.com

Available from all good bookshops or send a cheque to: Pocket Essentials
(Dept SS), P.O. Box 394, Harpenden, Herts, AL5 1XJ. Please make cheques
payable to 'Oldcastle Books', add 50p for postage and packing for each book
in the UK and £1 elsewhere.

Customers worldwide can order online at www.pocketessentials.com